Differentiated Leadership

Leadership for the Whole School

By Randy Thompson

Incentive Publications, Inc.
Nashville, Tennessee

Illustrated by Kathleen Bullock
Cover by Robert Voigts
Edited by Jill Norris
Copy-edited by Cary Grayson

ISBN 978-0-86530-715-5

1   2   3   4   5   6   7   8   9   10   11   10   09   08

PRINTED IN THE UNITED STATES OF AMERICA
www.incentivepublications.com

Table of Contents

All change is incremental, and differentiated leadership requires understanding how to move a diverse staff forward. Administrators need a model of change that will work for the entire staff. This model of change is based on the level of involvement of each staff member throughout the change process. Using the Involvement Model of Change will help administrators ensure that the staff is onboard and ready for what is ahead.

Differentiated leadership requires that leaders identify the various systems in their school and understand how those systems interact with each other. In this chapter, administrators will recognize the eight school performance management systems (SPMS) that are in every school, and how the systems are interdependent on each other. This chapter will walk administrators through a planning process that will take into account the impact any proposal will have on all of the School Performance Management Systems. This will eliminate the unintended consequences that often happen when implementing new programs.

All administrators work with a wide variety of groups, and each of the groups are made up of a wide variety of members. Since no two groups are the same, administrators need practical strategies for dealing with the group dynamics. This chapter is set up to be both diagnostic and prescriptive. Various group situations are described, and strategies for dealing with those situations are shared.

Differentiated leadership is about building collaborative systems of student management. In this chapter, administrators will see how to develop staff ownership of the student management process. The trick is to find ways for teachers with good student management skills to help the teachers with not-so-good student management skills. See how to get the teachers sharing strategies and assessing each other's discipline referrals in a nonthreatening collaboration.

For differentiated systems such as instruction, assessment, and so on, to occur, the administrative team has to develop a master schedule to allow these things to happen. In this chapter, the most flexible schedules are shared to assist administrators with this task.

In this chapter, administrators will see how to design staff activities using the multiple intelligences to motivate all of the staff members. We ask teachers to differentiate instruction, using strategies like multiple intelligence theory. Now administrators can differentiate leadership in the same way!

Administrators have long struggled with getting teachers to develop integrated curriculums that share standards and skills across content areas. This chapter has a very easy-to-implement system that will get teachers sharing instruction across content areas in meaningful ways. The key to the success of this system is its simplicity, and administrators can facilitate differentiated curriculum development that involves the whole school.

All administrators understand the need for community and business involvement, but often do not have the time or resources to put into it. In this chapter, administrators will find another easy-to-use program for developing meaningful community and business involvement in their school. The program is called COMPASS (an acronym for **COM**MUNITY **P**ARTNERSHIPS **A**SSURING **S**TUDENT **S**UCCESS), and you will see ways to create levels of community and business support that were not possible before this system.

Administrators will learn how to design engaging, interactive, and motivating staff meetings. Several staff meeting activities designed to present topics in a differentiated format are introduced in this chapter. The planning process and forms to help administrators create differentiated staff meetings are shared.

Do not run for the dictionary! The cognaffective school is a school where an equal emphasis is placed on the development of cognitive skills as well as affective skills. As this chapter demonstrates, every strategy shared in this book has blended the development and use of cognitive skills with the development and use of affective skills. The blending of the cognitive and the affective is the ultimate definition of differentiated leadership and is the only way to achieve leadership for the whole school.

Introduction

We all now have a pretty clear understanding of what is meant by differentiated instruction. The idea of differentiated instruction is to apply the most current brain-based research to the design of lessons to accommodate and motivate the various types of learners in each classroom. This requires that teachers have an understanding of the learning modalities and multiple intelligences to create lessons that captivate and engage all of the students. Differentiated instruction most simply is teaching the whole student. When teachers design lessons for the whole student, they design lessons for all students. In the spirit of recognizing diverse learners and providing instruction for them, I want school leaders to see that they can differentiate leadership.

Every school has staff members with diverse motivations, skill levels, and interests. Differentiated leadership is using the knowledge of brain-compatible learning and applying it to the staff, as well as to the students. Some teachers have stronger student management skills or curriculum development skills, while others have strengths in lesson design or are more creative. Some teachers have very good people skills and relate well with students and parents; but others—not so much. Savvy administrators create ways to stimulate staff participation in programs that take advantage of their learning preferences and offer opportunities for continuous professional growth.

In Chapter 6, I share how to develop activities that will motivate staff members to participate. When there are activities and assignments that appeal to each of the multiple intelligences, administrators will find greater staff participation and ownership. I even have a chapter to demonstrate how administrators can differentiate staff meetings. When administrators design activity systems for the whole teacher, they design activities and systems for the whole school.

This book is about practical applications for leaders. Every chapter in this book has strategies to demonstrate how administrators can make accommodations and modifications to motivate and develop every staff member. Some staff members (*"Negative Nelly," "Rumor Mill Rudy,"* or, my personal favorite, *"Karl Came with the Building"*) are perceived as antagonists and seem to be against anything new or different. What I have found is that when I can put Karl, Rudy, and Ms. Nelly in the correct situations, they become positive contributors to the school.

Differentiated leadership is about creating systems in the school that motivate and actively engage all of the stakeholders. Administrators need to understand and plan for the interaction within, and between, all of the systems in the school. In Chapter 2, leaders will see the eight school performance management systems. Planning for each of the systems is often done in isolation and without considering the impact a change in one system might have on the other systems. Administrators will see how the systems in the school interact, and how to plan for all of the systems simultaneously. There are easy-to-use forms and other tools provided for school leaders to help them differentiate the planning process.

Administrators that practice differentiated leadership find ways to transform the systems in their building into learning systems. A learning system is a system where, as the system carries out its purpose or function, the participants in the system also learn and grow professionally. For example, one of the purposes of the student management system in most schools is administering the student code of conduct and dealing with disciplinary issues. For the student management system to also be a learning system, everyone involved must freely provide and receive feedback in a way that allows for individual and cumulative growth. If continual feedback with sharing and learning are built into the system, so is self-assessment. Since the members of the system are continually learning and improving, the system constantly becomes more effective. Learning systems are designed to continually improve and become self-perpetuating.

Administrators will see that all the systems I share in this book are designed to be learning systems. For example, in the chapter on student management, I share two systems that enable staff members and administrators to share disciplinary issues and specific strategies. The systems I will share in Chapter 4 demonstrate how to get staff members interested in each other's referrals and then willing to share strategies for situations as they arise. After receiving input from other staff members and administrators, teachers can make better decisions regarding discipline. Likewise, the administrators will receive the feedback they need to ensure that discipline is being handled consistently across the school.

Another aspect of differentiated leadership is the grouping and regrouping of staff members to investigate and accomplish tasks. These groups include, but are certainly not limited to, departments, academies, teams, various school improvement committees, as well as parent and community groups. The diversity of the individual members of groups and of the groups themselves generate another set of challenges for administrators in creating and maintaining productive groups.

The purpose of Chapter 3, "Group Dynamics," is to assist administrative teams in managing groups. The leaders and group members will see how groups change from simple gatherings of individuals into working and productive groups. I have included several scenarios the administrators are sure to face when working with the various groups in their building. Each scenario demonstrates possible issues that cause dysfunction within the group. With each scenario, leaders will be given the probable causes for that type of situation, along with suggestions for working the group through each particular issue.

In the last chapter, I share how all of the strategies in this book are practices that lead to cognaffective schools. Yes, I know that cognaffective is not a word, and you probably see that I created it by combining the words cognitive and affective. A cognaffective school is a school in which an equal focus is placed on the development of both cognitive and affective skills. There is a more detailed description of the balance between cognitive and affective skill development in the cognaffective school in the last chapter.

I wanted to share this information here in the introduction because the affective skills of staff members are at least as critical as the cognitive skills. For example, a person having a great knowledge of such things as content or policies and procedures is only an asset if that person collaborates well with any of the other staff members, relates effectively to students, and understands clearly the process of learning. It is the combination of cognitive and affective skills that allows staff members to be most productive. Differentiated leadership is about developing the learning systems that allow the whole teacher to flourish by continuing to learn and grow professionally and personally. The cognaffective school requires differentiated leadership because it requires leadership for the whole school.

As leaders will see in Chapter 7, "Differentiated Curriculum Development," the system for curriculum development requires that teachers be content specialists and collaborate with teachers from other content areas. The way the process is set up, it enables administrators to help teachers learn from each other and continuously improve their content knowledge as well as their collaborative skills. The same goes for community and business involvement in Chapter 8. I will present a system for developing community and business involvement by differentiating the ways that partnerships can be developed. The process I will share appeals to the diverse skill sets used in each business, and allows each business to select the type of participation that fits the applications for their particular business. The reason these two systems and all of the others in this book work is because they are simple in practice and impressive in product.

Finally, this book is for anyone given leadership responsibilities or anyone interested in leadership and the impact of leadership on school performance. I will use the terms *administrator, leader, the leadership,* and *the administrative team* interchangeably in this book. These terms are meant to refer to any person in a leadership position for which the circumstances apply. For example, in the curriculum development chapter, all of the references to leadership in any form could mean any or all of the following: principals, assistant principals, district curriculum leaders, team leaders, department chairpersons, teacher leaders, curriculum committee members.

This book is not a scholarly presentation of leadership research, but rather a very practical application of the research that has been done by many others. People that are in leadership positions in education at any level are faced with incredible challenges every day. (And I do mean every day!) Leaders have no choice but to take the job with them everywhere they go. So this book is to help all leaders in education, at all levels, by giving them a few more tools for their tool chests.

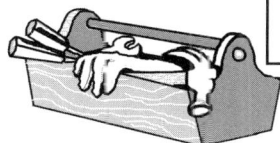

> *"If the only tool you have is a hammer, then everything looks like a nail."*
> *– Mark Twain*

The Involvement Model of Change

I am sure you are familiar with the expression that trying to lead change in schools is like trying to change the tires on a car, while it is still moving! We know what we want to do, but we can't ever quite catch up to it, and, if we did, it would be pretty hard to get the tool on the lug nuts. The other popular comparison to being a leader in education is that it is much like herding cats! No matter how you say it, leadership in schools today is a tremendous challenge.

One of the biggest jobs any leader does is getting everybody going in the same direction.

One of the biggest jobs of any leader is getting everyone on the staff going in the same direction at any one time. Administrative teams have to be able to work with our staffs to develop and communicate a common vision. Then the decisions have to be made for the best ways to proceed. The trick is getting everyone invested in the process so that they will do whatever it takes for success. In this chapter, I am going to share some very practical strategies for achieving consensus and making the required site-based decisions.

When the direction is determined with the staff, and everyone is in alignment, the training needed for the staff to accomplish the tasks required has to be identified and provided. This requires appropriate initial in-service to get the staff ready, and then adequate follow-up training to ensure that successful implementation is maintained. Follow-up training with continuous monitoring and adjusting assures the staff that the concept being implemented is here to stay. It is the continuous support that creates the conditions for success and builds the trust level with the staff.

Successful leaders are careful to develop staff ownership before moving ahead with any new concept or process. These leaders will actively involve the staff from the initial proposal, through the decision-making process and all the way to implementation. Leaders know they have been successful when the changes are not only implemented, but have become common practice. Every administrative team has to work with staff members of widely diverse talents, interests, and motivations. Differentiated leadership is about understanding how change occurs, and how to lead every member of the staff through any change.

The Six Steps of Change

Taking a new idea from concept to practice occurs in six steps. This is regardless of how simple or complex the new idea is. The six steps are described in detail later in this chapter and, as demonstrated by the chart below, are labeled according to level of involvement of the participants. As you will see later, trying to skip one of the steps pretty much always leads to problems. However, if administrative teams do follow the six steps, they will give themselves the best chances for success, and they will ensure they have "no teacher left behind"!

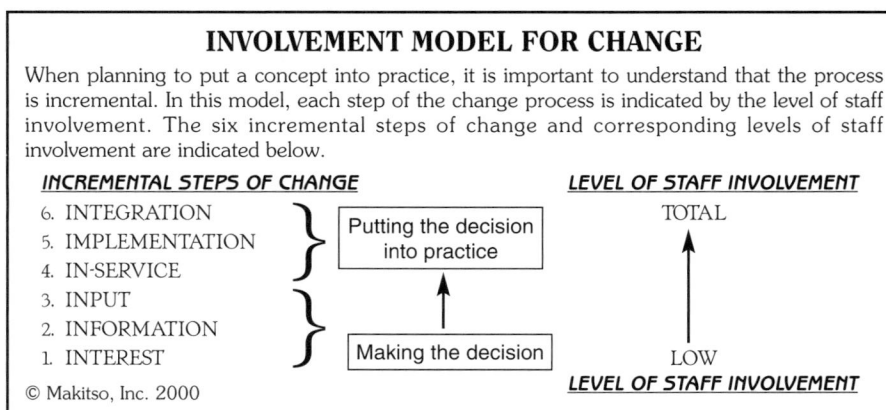

INVOLVEMENT MODEL FOR CHANGE

When planning to put a concept into practice, it is important to understand that the process is incremental. In this model, each step of the change process is indicated by the level of staff involvement. The six incremental steps of change and corresponding levels of staff involvement are indicated below.

INCREMENTAL STEPS OF CHANGE   **LEVEL OF STAFF INVOLVEMENT**

6. INTEGRATION   TOTAL
5. IMPLEMENTATION   } Putting the decision
4. IN-SERVICE   into practice
3. INPUT
2. INFORMATION   } Making the decision
1. INTEREST   LOW

© Makitso, Inc. 2000   **LEVEL OF STAFF INVOLVEMENT**

Interest

The change process begins when interest is generated by some potential action. Generating interest is the first step in introducing any type of change and is the lowest level of involvement for the staff. However, without some interest in the action, there is apathy, and the potential for success is dead in the water before it ever even gets going.

Interest can be generated in several ways and generally relate to some perception of need. The recognition of the need can come both internally and externally. For example, the recognition for the need for change may be external.

- The district office may relate that budgets are going to be cut district-wide by 15 percent, and your school is going to have to cut that amount from the budget for next year.

- The state may notify your school that the test scores for your school have not met the required measurements for success and will undertake some corrective action.

- The PTO or other parent organization may want to pursue the possibilities of implementing some programs.

On the other hand, the recognition for the need for change may be internal.

- Your school may decide to go through the accreditation process and generate several internal self-assessments to determine areas of strength and areas with needs for improvement.

- Your staff recognizes issues in the daily operations of the school. For example: too many students are in hallways during class, students are regularly tardy to class, or the lunches are not running very well due to time and discipline issues.

Teachers and administrators are often introduced to new concepts in many ways such as professional journals, attendance at professional conferences, and visitations to other schools. They may become interested in pursuing the idea and having it introduced schoolwide. Regardless of where it begins, the interest phase of change is time for exploring new ideas and possibilities.

This phase is the lowest level of involvement. It is the time for an initial introduction to the new idea and the changes it may imply. The interest may be forced as in the budget cut example above, or it may be voluntary as when it comes from a staff suggestion. Regardless, people that have some level of interest are ready for information to be provided. Once everyone has been introduced to an idea and has some understanding of why it is being considered, they are ready to actually study the idea and process the information, putting it into context.

Information

All decisions and actions are based on the information you have. Therefore it is absolutely critical that quality information be provided in a variety of ways to insure that the best decisions can be made. With enough information, there is universal understanding, and you can be certain that everyone is on the same page. That means we need to answer the age-old questions of *Who? What? When? Where? How?* and, perhaps most importantly, *Why?* Without adequate quality information, there is confusion, and the rumor mill has a field day!

The professional learning communities (PLCs) will undertake studies of the proposed concepts and/or actions being considered. Sometimes the study will initially explore the viability of the proposal and then move on to determining the best ways to put the proposal into practice. Other times there is no "if," as the decision has been made by the district. However, consideration must always be put into the best ways to carry out the decision.

The amount and the quality of the information provided can determine the eventual success (or lack thereof) for the implementation of changes. This is one area in which quality and quantity are both needed. There are many ways to get the information out, and administrators need to use a variety of means of communication since different staff members will absorb information in different ways. Administrators who communicate only via emails and staff meetings wonder why some staff members always seem to be misinformed. As with teaching a lesson, administrators need to focus on getting the information out in as many ways as possible. In doing so, we continually generate more INTEREST!

> ### Getting the Information Out!
> - Set up discussion or study groups, multimedia presentations, and presentations to small groups such as teams, academies, grade levels, or departments.
> - Provide literature to staff members.
> - Do book reviews.
> - Have guest speakers.
> - Provide graphics that breakdown key components.
> - Have the music people put information into a song.
> - Provide drawings, sketches, and diagrams to demonstrate concepts.

Input

It is critical that we get input from the stakeholders about their perceptions and understandings of the issues and changes being considered. As we gauge the level of understanding, we also determine the additional information required. We need to assess the amount of interest and the levels of understanding. Only when the input from staff indicates that they are ready, do we move forward.

Getting regular input from the staff ensures that administrators make decisions based on where the staff is. This also means that the ownership of the staff goes up dramatically since they know that their input is sought and valued. That means that the administrative team must have processes in place for gathering input from the staff and disaggregating the data as it comes in. Simply put, teachers need and want to give their input. If we do not have processes in place, it will happen informally and destructively.

For input to be valuable, it must be gathered from the widest base possible. Every individual needs to know that his or her opinion is being heard. We need to know how the various groups in the building are discussing the issues at hand, and we need to know where the rest of the administrative team is on the issues.

One building has their TLC for gathering input and disseminating certain types of information in the school. TLC stands for tender loving care, and is compromised of department chairs, team leaders, committee chairs, and members of the administrative team (including secretarial, custodial, and cafeteria staff). In this particular school, parents are represented on the TLC once a month. The TLC functions as their site-based, decision-making group. As such, this is where input is given since all factions in the school are represented. The school monitors and adjusts according to the input. We move forward when the input indicates the readiness of the staff.

During the input stage, leaders gauge interest and information levels and provide more of each as needed until the input shows the school is ready to move forward. Most of the schools I work with like to use a two-thirds majority vote to indicate when staff is ready to move forward. If the school is not yet at the two-thirds majority, they should continue to generate interest and provide the information needed to move the staff forward. It is very important to note that generating interest and providing information never stops.

In-Service/Planning

In this step, it is time to get the staff ready for what is ahead. The administrative team has worked through the first three steps to ensure that the staff is on board. Now they need to make sure the staff has the support to move ahead. In some instances, as in creating a new staff or student recognition system, there is little training and more planning to lay out the specifics of the system. The training involves having the staff that worked on the program share the particulars and answer questions. This process continues until the rest of the staff feels comfortable implementing the new recognition system.

In this step it also very important to include how the administrative team will assess the progress of the concept during the implementation. Information must be gathered for monitoring so that if adjustments are required, they are made in a timely manner, and with everyone anticipating their arrival. This will be discussed in the next step.

Also in this step, the plans are made for implementation, which most often will require some training. Training is the key to success in any organization, and it is critical in education. Do not confuse getting adequate information with training. The information and input stages are "talking about it" stages. Now it is time to train the staff to a level of comfort and competence that ensures they will be able to implement the change with success. Without proper training, the resulting confusion and lack of confidence combine to create high anxiety among staff members as they try to implement the change. Poor training almost always ensures poor performance, which severely limits the possibilities for success.

In-service is where the staff moves from theory into practice. The administrative team facilitates the move from the explanation, discussion, and decision phases of the change, to the demonstration and practice phase to get the staff ready to implement the change. *(As a trainer, I can tell you that this is not the time for theory. This is the time for very practical training. The training should actively engage the staff with modeling and practicing to develop the skills they will need to perform the tasks that will be expected of them.)*

Good training instills confidence as the staff realizes they are really prepared to take on the new challenges. Poor or no training creates apprehension for the staff because they have not had the opportunity to practice with the new concept. Also, the more training a person receives, the more invested they become in the project. The time that is put into training up front will be well worth the investment.

There is no substitute for bringing expert trainers to work with the staff; however, there are many books and materials available to assist administrative teams in providing in-service for their staffs. In the appendix of this book, I have listed several of the books and materials that would be good additions to the administrative team library for providing activities for in-house training. I am also going to share in the chapter on staff meetings several great activities for "mini in-service."

Differentiated Leadership
Copyright ©2008 by Incentive Publications, Inc., Nashville, TN.

It is also very important to remember to keep in mind the first three steps as a part of the training and planning. Maintaining the interest level and continuing to gain information is usually built into the training and planning processes. The administrative team needs to continue to receive input from the staff about their readiness. In this case, it is not the readiness to pursue the new concept, but rather the readiness to implement the new concept. Leaders need to assess the training and planning to determine with staff input when they are ready to proceed.

Implementation

If the first four steps have been done appropriately, implementation is generally the easiest part of the change process. There is usually a high level of excitement and anticipation to put the training to use. For the implementation to be successful, it is important to note that the administrative team will actually need to continue with the first four steps. Now the leaders' interest is in assessing the progress of the new concept. During implementation, the administrative team needs to be very active in monitoring how the implementation is progressing. That means the leaders are going to have to get input from the staff to know what adjustments, if any, might be required.

The administrative team needs to receive input from as many different perspectives as is possible. Therefore, the new concept should be a regular topic for meetings of any groups for which it would be appropriate. For example, the progress of the concept should be a topic of discussion at all administrative team meetings, all departmental meetings, all team meetings (if your school has teams), any appropriate committees, and so on, for the initial time of implementation. The methods of assessing and receiving input should be a part of the in-service/planning in the previous step. The administrative team should plan to have checkpoints predetermined, and formalize how they are going to receive input and publish that information. Continual monitoring and adjusting will keep misperceptions and unwanted practices from becoming a part of the program.

In-service takes on new meaning during implementation as the staff is now in the middle of putting the concept into practice. Staff members can ask more technical questions about procedures because they can reflect on what they have actually done throughout the initial implementation. Before, the questions were theoretical, as in "What do we do if this happens?" Now the questions are related to things that have actually happened in practice. That is why continued training is also critical. Not only does follow-up training clarify situations and keep bad habits from becoming practice, it also demonstrates the commitment and support of the administrative team to the staff.

Integration

Integration occurs when the new concept or idea becomes common practice. It is important for the administrative team to demonstrate their commitment to support the new idea or concept after it is implemented to ensure that it becomes common practice. Generally speaking, a concept or idea does not survive the vetting process of the first four steps unless it is has proven to be of value to the school. However, regardless of the value to the school, you hear many teachers say things like "This will never last!" and "We did this before, and we will do it again!" What they are actually saying is that in education things seem to come and go, and very few things actually stand the test of time. The things that do stand the test of time have achieved integration.

Achieving integration requires constant attention to the first five steps listed here. Losing interest is a quick way to see something end. When the administrative team continues to demonstrate interest, and works to generate new interest, the same usually goes for the staff. One great way to keep interest levels up is by continuing to provide new information to staff. Another way to maintain interest and get the latest information is for the administrative team to take staff members to professional conferences.

The administrative team also needs to continue to get input from the staff regarding the maintaining of the concept (now that it is no longer new). When the staff realizes that the leaders are continuing to solicit feedback about the concept, they know the concept is not going away. When the teachers think the administrative team is no longer interested, it is easy for them to lose interest as well.

Continuing to dedicate in-service time to the concept also ensures that it stays fully integrated in the school program. Schools should regularly review programs in the building to assess their level of integration and current viability. It will be necessary to revisit the first five steps for all programs at various times for them to remain vital. It is by continuing to review and move through this process that we keep programs from becoming those infamous "sacred cows"!

Staff members know that this program is not exempt from criticism and take ownership for making it the best it can be.

It is the continual cycling through the first five steps that maintains the motivation needed for integration.

> *Sacred cows*
> *make*
> *the best burgers!*
>
> – *Robert Kriegel*

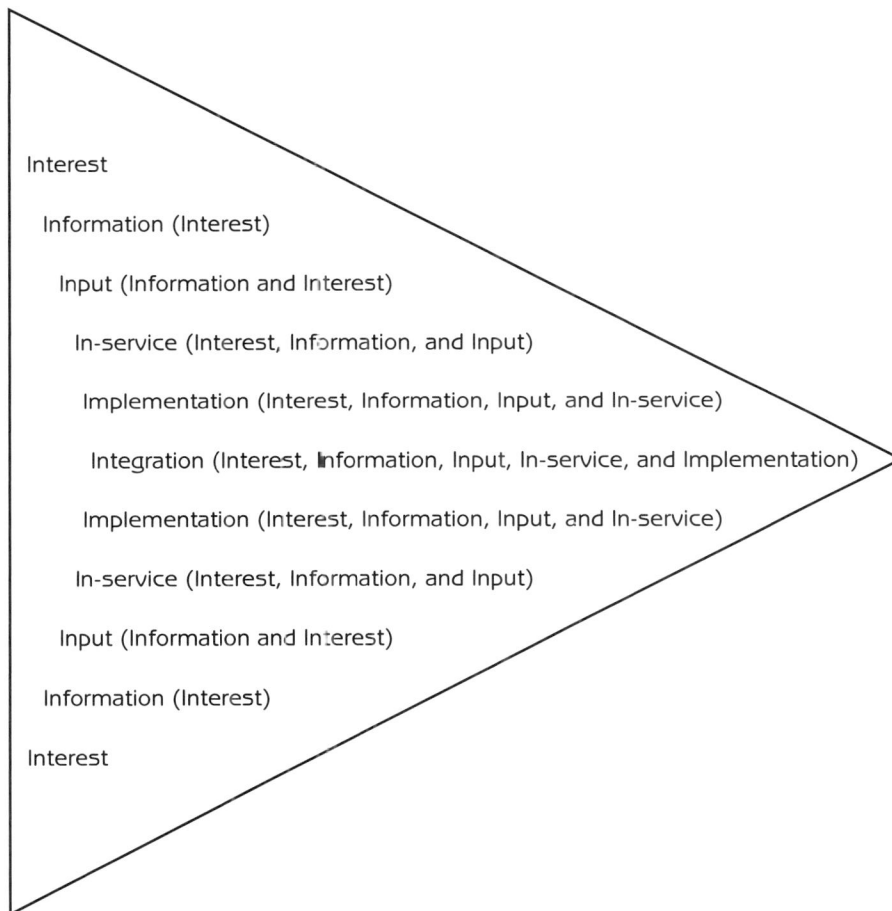

Interest

Information (Interest)

Input (Information and Interest)

In-service (Interest, Information, and Input)

Implementation (Interest, Information, Input, and In-service)

Integration (Interest, Information, Input, In-service, and Implementation)

Implementation (Interest, Information, Input, and In-service)

In-service (Interest, Information, and Input)

Input (Information and Interest)

Information (Interest)

Interest

This graphic demonstrates that getting an idea or process from concept to full integration requires interest, information, regular input for assessment, initial training, and continued follow-up training. Maintaining this or any program also requires continually generating interest, providing information, soliciting input for assessment, and continued follow-up training. All programs will be repeatedly cycling through these phases and should be assessed accordingly.

Involvement Model of Change

Steps in the Process

Level of Involvement

	Interest	Information	Input	In-Service	Implementation	Integration	Results
Total							
Integration	Interest	Information	Input	In-Service	Implementation	Integration ○	Loss of trust as concepts come and go, but few stay
Implementation	Interest	Information	Input	In-Service	Implementation ○	Integration	Spinning wheels and frustration
In-Service	Interest	Information	Input	In-Service ○	Implementation	Integration	No training = staff anxiety and poor performance
Input	Interest	Information	Input ○	In-Service	Implementation	Integration	No investment or ownership, but much resistance
Information	Interest	Information ○	Input	In-Service	Implementation	Integration	Rumor mill and confusion about what is being considered
Interest	Interest ○	Information	Input	In-Service	Implementation	Integration	Staff apathy, no motivation, and a nonstarter
Low							

Model of Change Chart

This chart demonstrates the level of involvement of the staff as it relates to the six steps of change that the staff will have to move through to take a new idea or process from being a concept to becoming common practice. Particular attention should be paid to the results of not giving enough attention to any of the steps. It is also important to remember that as the level of involvement increases with each phase of the change process, it also becomes increasingly important to continue to focus on each of the previous steps, as each increment is dependent on the continuation of the previous steps.

Model of Change Planning Form

Administrative teams can use the form below (or create a similar form of your own) to plan for each phase of the change process, remembering that each step is indicated by staff's level of involvement. The chart calls for leaders to keep in mind that each step is dependent on the continuation of the previous steps. That is why each previous step is included as a part of the planning of each step.

Integration	Notes: (Implementation): (In-service): (Input): (Information): (Interest):	Trust is established by achieving this level. Now trust must be maintained with constancy, input, and assessment. Keep staff focused, and regenerate interest and motivation with follow-up training.
Implementation	Notes: (In-service): (Input): (Information): (Interest):	Information needs to be shared through previously established systems to regularly assess success. Follow-up "training in progress" continues. Input from staff will drive any adjustments and the ongoing in-service.
In-service and Planning	Notes: (Input): (Information): (Interest):	Training ensures staff skills and increases confidence. Input and information are needed to assess and receive feedback to gauge staff readiness. Plan for feedback during implementation for monitoring and adjusting.
Input	Notes: (Information): (Interest):	Solicit staff input to gauge staff ownership and knowledge; continue to generate interest and information until consensus is reached.
Information	Notes: (Interest):	Gather and share info in a variety of ways to expose the staff to the new concept and keep them interested.
Interest	Notes:	Generate interest and motivate the staff to look into a new concept.

At-Your-Fingertips Reference

INVOLVEMENT MODEL FOR CHANGE

When planning to put a concept into practice, it is important to understand that the process is incremental. In this model, each step of the change process is indicated by the level of staff involvement. The six incremental steps of change and corresponding levels of staff involvement are indicated below.

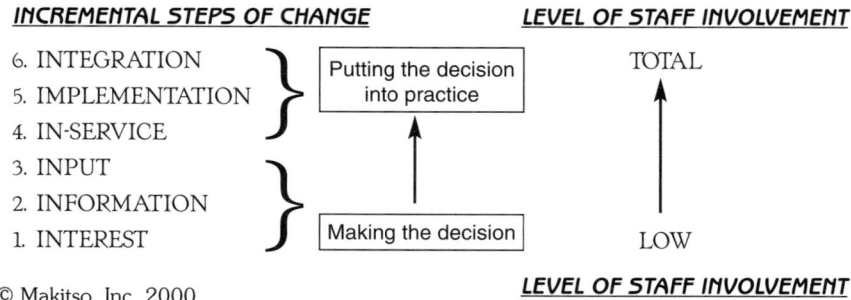

INCREMENTAL STEPS OF CHANGE

6. INTEGRATION
5. IMPLEMENTATION
4. IN-SERVICE
3. INPUT
2. INFORMATION
1. INTEREST

Putting the decision into practice

Making the decision

LEVEL OF STAFF INVOLVEMENT

TOTAL

LOW

LEVEL OF STAFF INVOLVEMENT

© Makitso, Inc. 2000

1. Interest: Enough interest has to be generated to warrant further investigation and investment in a new idea or process. A process is in place for staff interests to be shared and developed. This might include dedicating time for new ideas to be shared in staff meetings, department meetings, team meetings, a staff-only newsletter, or study groups. Failing to generate interest results in apathy. This is why many concepts never get off the ground.

2. Information: Quality information about the new idea or process has to be generated and shared in a variety of ways with all staff. Investigation into the new concept is done through the meetings, study groups, and newsletters. Generating this information is an important step to making knowledgeable decisions. Failing to provide many opportunities to gain information in a variety of ways about the proposed concept allows for rumors and misinformation to jeopardize the project. Continue to generate interest at this level.

3. Input: In this step, the staff will give their input, and a decision will be made about the proposed concept. Staff feedback is critical to assess its level of understanding and readiness for making the decision. There must be a process in place for gathering staff input, and decision making. Staff input in the decision-making process guarantees more ownership in the new concept or process. As a staff moves through the first three levels of involvement, they are taking ownership of the concept. Continue to gather information.

4. In-Service and Planning: Being well informed about the idea is not the same as being trained to have the skills for "walking the walk." Some things, like a new reward program, may not require training, but will require careful planning before starting. Adequate training and planning is critical for successful implementation of the concept or process. A lack of training or planning can lead to staff anxiety and poor implementation. Continued training will ensure staff readiness and success. Continue to get input to assess readiness to implement.

5. Implementation: In this step, the change is put into practice. During implementation, training takes on new importance since all staff members are now actually engaged and making adjustments as needed. Failing to implement the concept leads to frustration and the feeling of spinning one's wheels. Continue to train, monitor, and adjust.

6. Integration: The idea or process moves from concept to become an integral part of the expectations and operational systems of the school. The concept is now common practice and a central part of normal operations. Failure to follow through leads to a loss of trust as concepts come and go, with few staying. Continue to address all of the previous levels to keep the practice current.

TAG . . . You're It!

Using the Involvement Model of Change

Exercise One:

The administrative team should take a current proposal and use the planning chart on page 19 to discuss how the proposal might be taken from concept to common practice.

Exercise Two:

The administrative team should list several programs that are in some stage of implementation. Use the planning chart on page 19 to identify the stages of implementation of the various programs. Then discuss how the administrative team is going to continue to support the program. For example, suppose there is an advisory program in the building and the teachers actually have to implement the activities for the program for the first time this year. Using the chart, the questions would be:

- How is the program being assessed?

- How are the teachers giving their input?

- How often is input expected?

- How is information continuing to be distributed and collected?

- Is the interest level still high?

- What in-service is needed to further the teachers' confidence and abilities with the program?

- Did the previous in-service prove adequate?

- Is the program proceeding as planned?

- What adaptations or modifications are needed?

- Where would the administrative team place the program on the continuum toward integration?

School Performance Management Systems

Introduction

Differentiated leadership requires that leaders identify the various systems in their charge and understand how those systems interact with each other. The major *school performance management systems* (SPMS) are shown in the diagram below.
(I have found that these eight systems have worked well for planning purposes, and as an administrator, I liked to have a group/committee that was responsible for any considerations for each one of the SPMS.)

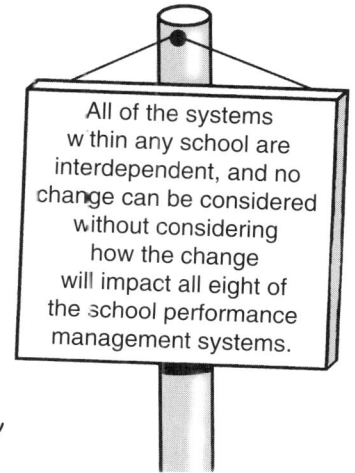

All of the systems within any school are interdependent, and no change can be considered without considering how the change will impact all eight of the school performance management systems.

Any new proposals or other operational issues that come up are run through all eight systems for planning purposes. It is most important that administrative teams understand that all of the systems within any school are interdependent, and no change can be considered without considering how the change will impact all eight of the school performance management systems. Any change in one of the systems will have a ripple effect on all of the systems, whether intended or not. Therefore, trying to effect change in one of the systems without simultaneously working in the other systems greatly increases the likelihood for failure.

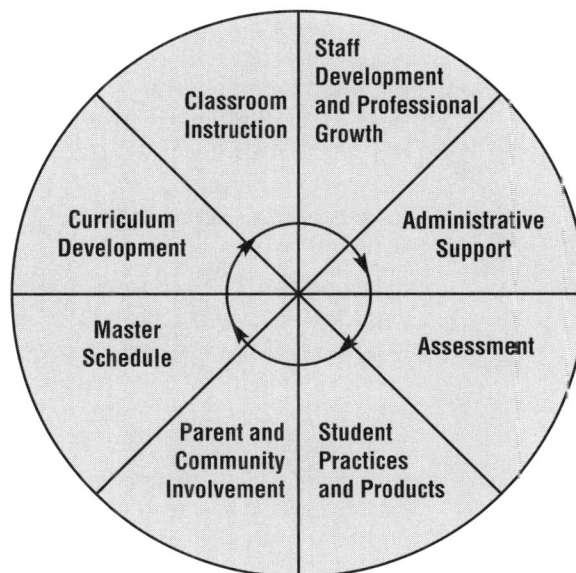

Failing to consider all of the SPMS in planning is the reason why so many school change initiatives are not successful. For example, a school will implement a block schedule with no training for classroom instruction in the block, or preparation of the students for the block, or designing curriculum for the block, and so on. Then the school will blame failure of the implementation on the concept of block scheduling when it does not work. When the block schedule was being considered, the administrative team should have looked at what changes would be necessary in each of the other systems. Again, any change in one or more of the systems is always going to impact all of the other systems. Anticipating the impact a change will have on all of the systems, and then planning for it, can be the difference between success and failure.

In this chapter, I am going to share how to plan for the ripple effect that can create so much frustration. To eliminate the frustration, the right questions need to be asked early in the process of considering any changes. Of course, the first question is "What system or systems does the new proposal fit in?" A new proposal for a curriculum mapping process would most likely be first considered by the curriculum development group. Then the proposal would need to be considered in relation to the impact it will have on the other SPMS. In fact, I share this exact situation a little later in this chapter.

As you will also see later in this chapter, a new proposal for something like an advisory program is not going to fit into any one of the school performance management systems, and would need to be considered in multiple areas first. In this case, there would preferably be a group of the staff that was interested in advisory programs that would investigate them and present the school with a proposal for an advisory program. That proposal would then need to be considered in reference to all eight of the SPMS. This example of planning for an advisory program is discussed in more detail later, and is included as one of the exercises at the end of this chapter.

Regardless of the proposal, the administrative team will want to facilitate the brainstorming process across the school performance management systems in order to anticipate what the actual tasks are going to be within each of the systems, and thereby increase the likelihood of accomplishing the goal of the proposal. Before I discuss how the School Performance Management Systems (SPMS) are going to interact with each other, and how we will plan accordingly, I first need to share a couple of planning strategies that will assist leaders with every phase of planning.

Planning Strategies

The first strategy is for leaders to discuss and demonstrate personal responsibilities (PRs) with the staff. Staff members understand the idea of personal responsibilities, but should be reminded of personal responsibilities in the context of the functioning of any organization, and especially in the instance of schools. In organizations, meetings take place all the time, but the ultimate measure of success for any meeting is what takes place **after** the meeting. So many times, people leave meetings not sure what was accomplished and confused about who is supposed to do what. Personal responsibilities (PRs) are the responsibilities an individual takes on or is assigned. *That is why I recommend to administrative teams that any time a group in their building meets, the personal responsibilities should be summarized for each topic during the meeting. The PRs should then be summarized and clarified again at the close of the each meeting, and then published after the meeting for all those involved.*

With each topic at any meeting there are two questions that are nonnegotiable and absolutely must be asked. The first question is "What tasks will there be as a result of this topic?" The second question is "Who is going to be responsible for this task?"

If there are no tasks as a result of this topic, and no action is going to be taken, then I might question the need for the discussion in the first place. In schools with teams, I often sit in on team meetings where student behaviors are discussed, and the team will move on to other students with no actions being taken. Another example of an area of great discussion, but little action, is the dress code.

In these instances, the meeting is great for blowing off steam in what would very kindly be called a "gripe session." I am sure you know what I am talking about. I want somebody at that meeting, and in all meetings, to say something like: "We have discussed this student, and now what is actually going to be done?" I suggest that when a staff member brings an issue to a meeting, that staff member should be ready to offer suggestions for actions to be considered. Group members should be asking what tasks would be appropriate for this situation.

When I coach groups like disciplinary committees, academies, and teams, I have them state the issues as succinctly as possible and get into what they might be able to do about each issue as quickly as is reasonable. I have interrupted many team meetings at a lot of schools to say something like: "I do not even know this student, but I know what his issues are because they have been stated here several times. My question is, "What is going to be done?" You will see (in the Student Management chapter of this book) that I like to have lists available that show what the possible actions are for student management situations so the teachers can select the most appropriate one for each situation.

At the end of every meeting, the personal responsibilities should be summarized, and after the meeting the PRs should be published for all those concerned. This process makes it very clear who has personal responsibilities, and of course who does not. The administrative team, and for that matter anyone else, can quickly evaluate the distribution of the PRs among any group, and the staff as a whole.

Administrative teams will find that inequities among the staff regarding Personal Responsibilities will most often begin to even out pretty quickly as staff members become aware of the PRs. Some staff members think they are doing much more than they really are, and summarizing the PRs helps each staff member self-assess what his or her contributions are to their group. Most staff members truly want to be supportive and are willing to carry their weight with their group. This process helps the administrative team and staff members recognize when and where a little more motivation might be needed.

There are three areas or levels of personal responsibilities in every school. The three areas of PRs are group, organizational, and self. Every person will have personal responsibilities from all three areas and, as is often the case, some PRs will overlap and be in two or all three areas of responsibility.

Group Responsibilities

These are the responsibilities assigned to any subgroup of the organization. In a school, these would, of course, include interdisciplinary academies or teams, departments, committees, the faculty, parent organizations, and so on. These responsibilities might include things like academies or teams developing common policies and dealing with student management issues as a group. A department might be called on to decide on a new textbook series, or to develop differentiated lessons and assessments. This might also include parent organizations, business partnership groups, school improvement committees, and on and on, since most schools have numerous groups with a variety of functions.

The group personal responsibilities an individual might have would be to those groups in the school in which he or she is a member. These PRs would include such things as actively participating in committee, academy, or team meetings; evaluating textbooks for a departmental review and selection of new textbooks; or mapping your part of the curriculum for integrating the curriculum. For an administrator, group PRs might include such things as working on district level committees, participating in parent organization meetings, and facilitating the administrative team meetings.

Organizational Responsibilities

These are the responsibilities assigned to the entire organization and often the leadership. For a school, this would include carrying out the district and school mission statements; and this often entails providing a safe learning environment and quality instruction with appropriate facilities. For the leaders of a school, these responsibilities are usually such things as master schedule development, overseeing the budget process, carrying out the district evaluation process, and managing the systems within the school.

The organizational PRs that a person has are to those organizations to which he or she belongs. When the organization is a school, these personal responsibilities might include such things as following the district curriculum guide, attending parent nights and board meetings, and getting grades in on time. For an administrator, these responsibilities might include doing classroom observations or handling discipline referrals.

Self Responsibilities

The self PRs that a person might have would include, but certainly not be limited to, things like an individual's personal and professional growth. This would include such things as preparation for classes, maintaining certifications, attaining advanced degrees, and individual research of personal interest. This would also include personal growth, such as pursuing individual hobbies and interests, and so on.

Group and organizational responsibilities are only accomplished by the individuals that make up the groups and organizations. Individuals must carry out their own personal responsibilities. That is why it is critical not just to speak of the group's responsibilities, but also to list and publish the personal responsibilities that must be completed in order to complete the group's responsibilities. The same goes for the organization. This way people cannot hide in or behind the groups they work with. Either they have taken on PRs or they have not; and if these are always a prominent part of all discussions, there is built-in accountability.

Target of Involvement

Another strategy is for leaders to use the target-of-involvement organizer shown below, which is a brainstorming tool that works well for groups in most discussion sessions. The goal is stated in the middle of the target. Then when someone recommends a task that needs to be done to reach the goal, his or her suggestion is written in one of the circles of the target. Groups also record personal responsibilities and a timeline in the rings for each task. Everyone in the group needs to know who is responsible to do what and when it is to be completed.

To use the planning tool, the group will identify the target goal, and write it in the center of the target. Then the group will brainstorm the tasks to be done to accomplish the goal, and write each task in a ring of the target. With each task the group should also identify the personal responsibilities and set a timeline for completing the tasks. Groups should add as many rings as needed to list all of the tasks required to accomplish the target goal.

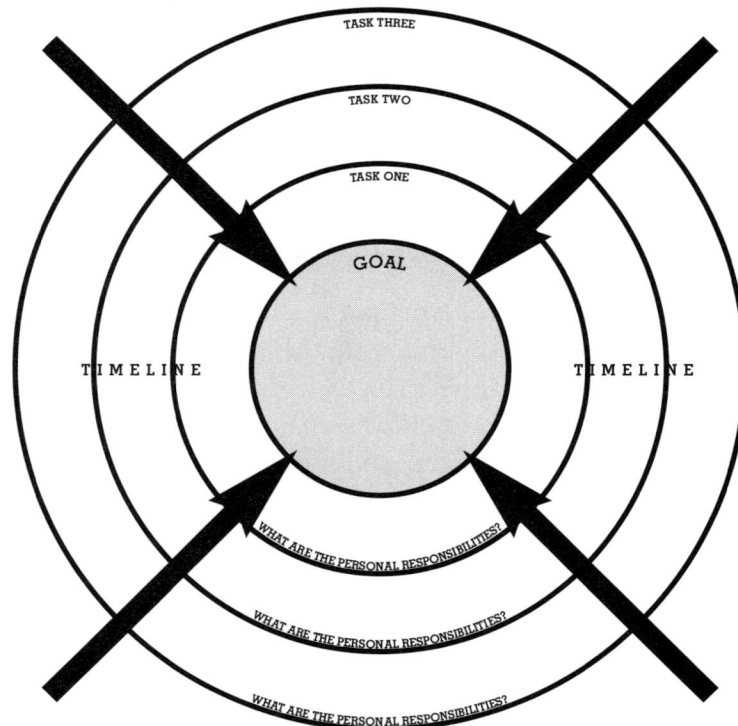

TASK THREE

TASK TWO

TASK ONE

GOAL

TIMELINE   TIMELINE

WHAT ARE THE PERSONAL RESPONSIBILITIES?

WHAT ARE THE PERSONAL RESPONSIBILITIES?

WHAT ARE THE PERSONAL RESPONSIBILITIES?

Differentiated Leadership

Planning for School Performance Management Systems (SPMS)

The school performance management systems (SPMS) are integrally interdependent, and no system should ever be discussed in isolation. Every decision made in one system will have some ripple effect in the other systems. Differentiated leadership means that leaders are going to anticipate the impacts to all systems and plan accordingly. The first task with any new proposal is to determine which system is initially affected and establish the tasks that will be required within that system to achieve the goal of the new proposal.

For example, suppose the curriculum leadership has proposed initiating a curriculum mapping process with the initial goal being to develop cross-curriculum, interdisciplinary learning connections, and with a long-term goal to develop cross-curriculum, interdisciplinary student projects. In many schools, this task would be left to the curriculum leaders only, and they would work with the staff to begin the mapping process. Differentiated leadership calls for the leaders to consider all of the possible implications.

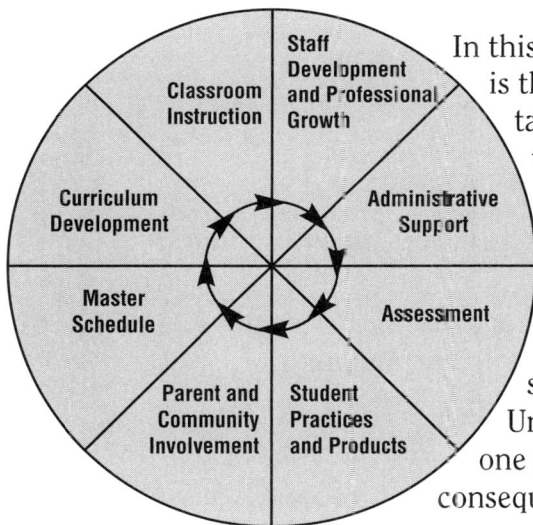

In this example, curriculum development is the area where the initial proposal is taking place. First, list what is going to have to happen to make the curriculum changes that are proposed. Then, consideration must be given to the ripple impact the curriculum changes are going to have on each of the other systems. These will also be listed. Unless carefully planned, changes in one system may create unintended consequences in the other systems.

For example, suppose the administrative team is going to look at the proposed curriculum changes. The first task is to list the tasks that are likely to be needed in the curriculum area which is outlined following this section. Then they should consider the potential impacts these curriculum activities will have on the other systems that are listed on pages 31–33. The administrative team needs to understand that if the changes in curriculum call for changes in the other systems that cannot happen, then the changes in curriculum may not be as effective as they could be.

Curriculum Development

Goal: Initiate a curriculum mapping process with the initial goal being to develop cross-curriculum, interdisciplinary learning connections, and the long-term goal being cross-curriculum, interdisciplinary student projects. (See Chapter 7 on differentiated curriculum development for a detailed discussion and development of this goal.)

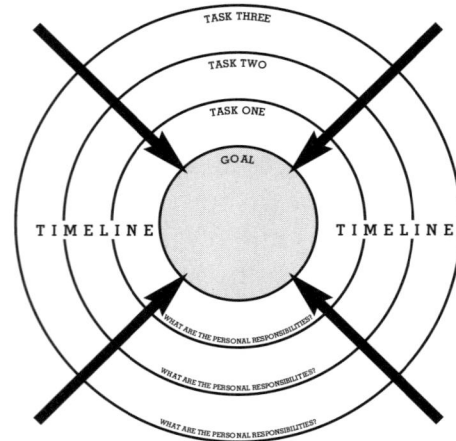

The tasks required are:

- **Build the maps by grade level.** *(If your school has academies, then also build the maps by academy or team.)*
  - ☐ Use curriculum and pacing guides to indicate major topics taught in each area
  - ☐ Build one exploratory map per grade level
  - ☐ Indicate the state standards and test items
  - ☐ Indicate the use of programs such as writing programs
  - ☐ Indicate media use and technology use
  - ☐ Indicate support programs

- **Realign instructional timelines and agree on curriculum as needed within departments.**
  - ☐ Use sample state test questions that have been put on the maps to indicate gaps in curriculum
  - ☐ Use disaggregated data to indicate areas of concern on the maps

- **Find learning connections across curriculum areas.**
  - ☐ Teachers look for descriptors that indicate skills taught in one area might also be used in another area

- **Discuss and develop learning connections.**
  - ☐ Teachers have to meet with teachers from other curriculum areas to develop such specifics of the learning connection as reference points, extra credit, shared overheads, worksheets, assignments, and assessments

- **Compass—develop a community-based curriculum.**
  - ☐ Use the COWs as a communication tool to help develop business partnerships

Differentiated Leadership
Copyright ©2008 by Incentive Publications, Inc., Nashville, TN.

Move through each of the systems beginning with
Curriculum Development.

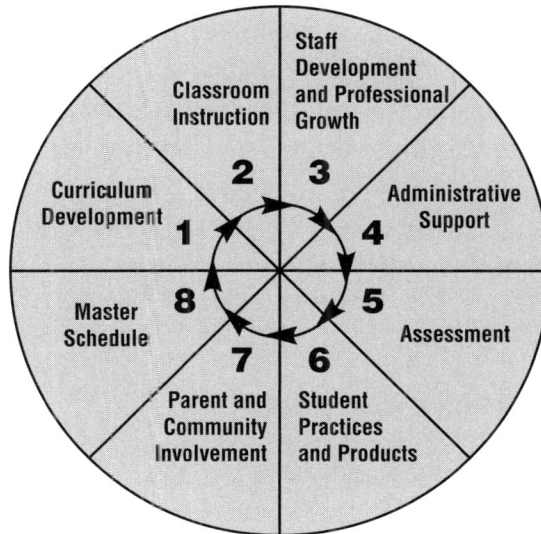

#1 Curriculum Development

The administrative team must consider what the impacts of those
changes will be on the other systems. A partial list is provided in each
area as examples of the impact the curriculum changes will have and of
the tasks that will be needed in each of the other systems.
*NOTE: The personal responsibilities and timelines are not included here,
but certainly should be on your lists.*

#2 Classroom Instruction

Teachers will need to:
- plan with teachers from other disciplines
- bring in activities from other content areas to use in
  their classroom to naturally differentiate instruction.
- work with other teachers to develop embedded themes
  and ongoing cross-curriculum projects
- be able to give grades for work done in other classes
- share worksheets, overheads/visuals, and activities
  between disciplines
- develop guided choice assignments based on topic in other areas
- give extra credit for work done in other classes that uses
  related skills
- share appropriate assessment items across curriculum areas

#3 Staff Development and Professional Development

- The teachers will need initial training for developing the curriculum maps and how to use them.
- The administrative team will need training for supporting the staff in the curriculum mapping process.
- Follow-up training should be provided to support the staff as they actually begin to discuss and develop learning connections.
- Additional training will be needed for the teachers and community members for **COMPASS** (**COM**munity **P**artnerships **A**ssuring **S**tudent **S**uccess). *(See Chapter 8 for more details.)*

#4 Administrative Support

The administrative team will need to:

- provide the training
- create the space for the maps and the meeting space for curriculum development
- provide release time, or other strategies for teachers from different content areas to meet
- use the maps to document initiatives and areas of concern
- cross-reference the state standards
- work with the departments to ensure curriculum alignment
- create a form of documentation for learning connections
- introduce the curriculum maps to local businesses which mean taking the maps to the business or a Chamber of Commerce meeting
- work with the teachers to develop community partnerships (COMPASS)

#5 Assessment

For this goal, administrators will need to assess:

- teacher participation (both core and exploratory)
- types of learning connections
- state standards included in learning connections
- the impact on classroom performance
- student performance on the state assessments
- administrative team support
- community participation

#6   Student Practices and Products

The students will be:
- doing worksheets and activities in classes that relate to other classes
- able to earn extra credit from multiple teachers for many assignments
- participating in cross-curriculum, long-term projects
- maintaining portfolios for their projects and for some assessments
- having grades on single assignments count in multiple classes

#7   Parent and Community Involvement

- Businesses and parents are exposed to the curriculum maps (at open houses, by invitation, at Chamber of Commerce meetings).
- The businesses will look at the maps to find areas where skills being taught correspond to skills used in the business.
- Someone from the business will have to meet with the teacher or teachers to discuss and develop the learning connection.
- Parents will also use the curriculum maps to look for learning connections based on skills that relate to their expertise.

#8   Master Schedule

To maximize curriculum mapping and developing learning connections, the master schedule will have to:
- accommodate interdisciplinary teaching teams (if your team has academies or teams)
- be flexible enough to allow for things like shared and authentic assessments
- allow for differentiated instruction, which often implies extended learning time, that can be accommodated with a flexible block schedule or some sort of an A–B rotating schedule

The lists above are partial views of the various tasks that might be required in each of the other systems given the changes proposed in curriculum development. These are all based on the tasks that were initially identified for the curriculum changes. So it is beneficial for the administrative team to use a tool like the target of involvement organizer (page 28) with the appropriate staff members (in this case the members of the curriculum development committee) to brainstorm any proposed changes and all of the tasks that will be involved as they relate to creating the new curriculum model. As a part of this process, this group will discover some of the tasks that will be required in the other systems, and they should list those, as is shown above.

At some point, this group would share their proposal for curriculum changes and their findings of the tasks involved with the rest of the staff. Then groups representing the other systems should take the proposal with the currently identified tasks and consider any additional impacts that might result from the proposed curriculum changes. Each group should use a tool, like the target of involvement, and brainstorm any additional tasks that might be required. It is important to remember to include the PRs and timelines for any tasks that are mentioned. I will share a form on page 13 that schools can use as a model to create a cumulative display of all the systems with all of the tasks, PRs, and timelines.

If your school does not already have committees established that cover the school performance management systems that are listed here, I would recommend that the administrative team consider doing so. Of course, your groups do not have to match the SPMS, but it is important that there are groups within the school that can consider how proposed changes will impact each of the systems. The chart on page 36 demonstrates how not considering each of the systems can affect school planning and performance.

When the groups have completed their initial tasks (those personal responsibilities and timelines would have been established above), they will come together to combine their findings. Some schools will use poster board or something similar to create displays demonstrating all of the tasks in all of the systems, with the PRs and timelines indicating how they all relate to each other. It is not hard to guess that, at this time, some adjustments will most likely be required. This part of the process helps eliminate conflicting timelines or PRs.

The form on the next page gives administrative teams a format for creating displays to consider the systems in relation to each other while evaluating a proposed change in one or more of the systems. This form is also contained in the "Differentiated Leadership Planner Foldout." Depending on the change, you might need individual sheets for each SPMS. Samples of these forms are on pages 54–57, and a form that can be used as an overall checklist is on page 53.

School Performance Management Systems and Levels of Personal Responsibility Planning Chart

Differentiated leadership means planning for the change-induced interaction between the management systems. After listing the impacts of a change on the management systems, list the various tasks and personal responsibilities that will be required for each of the systems. Use the target of involvement organizer to brainstorm the tasks and the personal responsibilities needed for each system, and list them here. This way it is easy to see what needs to be done, who is going to do it, and when it is going to happen.

Goal _____

School Management Systems:	Tasks	Personal Responsibilities Self/Group/Organizational	Timeline
Parent and Community Support			
Staff Development and Professional Growth			
Administrative Support			
Assessment			
Student Practices and Products			
Classroom Instruction			
Master Schedule			
Curriculum Development			

Curriculum Development	Master Schedule	Classroom Instruction	Student Practices and Products	Assessment	Administrative Support	Staff Dev. & Professional Growth	Parent and Community Involvement	Result if ONLY THE AREA MARKED WITH AN X is considered
X								Use of the same curriculums, with no content changes, no integration or collaboration between content areas, lack of alignment with standards, and so on.
	X							Schedule may not support programs like teaming, differentiated instruction, advisory, etc. No new flexibility, and so on.
		X						No change in instruction means "same old, same old" and no impact on student performance.
			X					Nothing changes from the student perspective or in practice, so no cognitive or affective achievement gains can be made.
				X				No way to measure success, no data to make decisions, no ability to monitor and adjust.
					X			Nonstarter without administrative support, budget, recourse, accountability, and so on.
						X		Staff is stagnant with much anxiety and resistance, poor performance, and so on.
							X	Poor public relations, loss of parent and community support, misinformation and rumors, and so forth.

Differentiated Leadership
Copyright ©2008 by Incentive Publications, Inc., Nashville, TN.

SPMS Planning

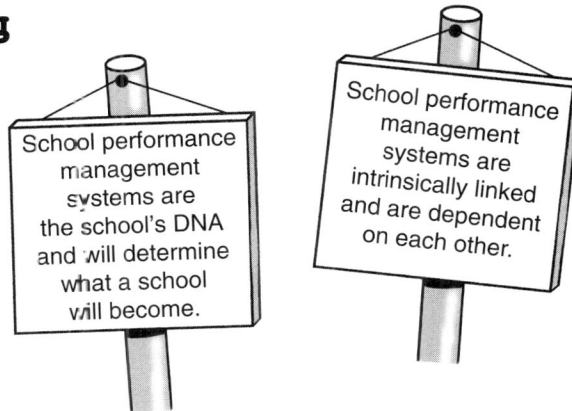

School performance management systems are the school's DNA and will determine what a school will become.

School performance management systems are intrinsically linked and are dependent on each other.

The chart on page 36 shows the results of SPMS planning when administration and staff members have not taken all the school performance management systems into consideration. Careful planning does not have to take long periods of time. If the discussion about a proposal is concise, and all areas are considered, it is probably not too hard to see that this process will actually save time in the long run. Good initial planning will create preparations that will anticipate most issues.

Consider how the results of the curriculum project would change if each of the eight systems are considered. In the following example, each system is highlighted separately. Each form indicates questions that address the change in the specific system and additional questions for each of the other areas in relation to the highlighted system. Below, I am going to demonstrate how to initiate the consideration of a proposal in each of the eight school performance management systems.

Curriculum Development

Questions to help begin the discussion, investigation, and consideration of new proposals for Curriculum Development might include:

Departmental

- Will the curriculum proposal involve all of the content areas? If not, which content areas will be involved?
- Will the curriculum proposal require new books or other materials?
- Will the curriculum proposal require a change in pacing guides?
- Will the curriculum proposal require realigning any or all of the curriculums?

Interdisciplinary

- Will the curriculum proposal require interdepartmental collaboration?
- What materials might be required for the new proposal?

**Curriculum Development Proposal's
Potential Impact on Other SPMS to be Considered**

Classroom Instruction

- Which of the content areas will be affected by this curriculum development?
- How will classroom instruction be impacted?
- Will the changes be departmental or interdisciplinary or both?

Staff Development

- Will the curriculum development require staff training?
- Will the curriculum development require any other training?

Administrative Support

- What will be the administrative responsibilities needed to implement the curriculum development proposal being considered?

Assessment

- What assessments will be needed to gauge staff readiness and the effectiveness of the curriculum development proposal being considered?
- Will this impact the state test objectives and national standards?
- Does the data support the curriculum development proposal?
- Will this action need to be noted on any of the school reports?
- What sort of data will need to be collected to assess this curriculum development proposal?

Parent and Community Involvement

- Will the proposed curriculum development changes need to be communicated to the community? If so, how is this to be accomplished?
- How will the curriculum development changes involve the community?

Student Practices and Products

- What will the students be doing differently as a result of the changes?
- How will student performance, practices, and products be impacted by the curriculum development proposal?

Differentiated Leadership
Copyright ©2008 by Incentive Publications, Inc., Nashville, TN.

Master Schedule
- Will the master schedule support the curriculum development changes?
- What changes might be needed in the master schedule to support the curriculum development proposal?

Classroom Instruction

Questions to help begin the discussion, investigation, and consideration of new proposals for classroom instruction might include:

How will classroom instruction be impacted by this action?
- What change in instruction can be expected?
- Will training be required for the change in classroom instruction?

What will teachers be "doing" in the classroom as a result of this action?

Who will be responsible for making any needed changes in classroom instruction?

Who will be responsible for materials, accountability, and training?

What classroom materials, if any, will be needed?

> ### Classroom Instruction Proposal's
> ### Potential Impact on Other SPMS to be Considered

Student Practices and Products
- How will student practices and products change as a result of the changes in classroom instruction?

Parent and Community Involvement
- How will parent and community involvement be impacted by the proposed changes in classroom instruction?

Staff Development and Professional Growth
- What staff development will be needed to implement the proposed changes in classroom instruction?

Administrative Support

- What administrative support will be required for the changes in classroom instruction?
- Who will be responsible for making any needed changes in classroom instruction?
- Who will be responsible for needed materials, accountability, and training?

Assessment

- How will the readiness and then the effectiveness of the proposed changes in classroom instruction be measured?
- How will the changes be assessed in regards to the state standards?
- Does the data support the proposal for classroom instruction?
- Who will be responsible for monitoring and assessing classroom instruction to ensure change has taken place?

Curriculum Development

- Will curriculum changes be required?
- Will the changes be departmental or interdisciplinary or both?

Master Schedule

- Will the master schedule support the changes being considered?
- What changes in the master schedule might be needed to support the classroom instruction being considered?

Staff Development and Professional Growth

Questions to help begin the discussion, investigation, and consideration of new proposals for staff development and professional growth might include:

- What staff development is being considered?
- What professional growth will there be as a result of this action?
- Do our current professional learning communities enable us to train and support the proposed action?
- Do new professional learning communities need to be created to support the proposed action?
- Who will be responsible for organizing the staff development?

Differentiated Leadership
Copyright ©2008 by Incentive Publications, Inc., Nashville, TN.

Staff Development and Professional Growth
Potential Impact on Other SPMS to be Considered

Classroom Instruction

- Will any of the content areas be affected by staff development?
- How will classroom instruction be impacted?

Parent and Community Involvement

- Will the community be involved in the staff development and professional growth, or need to be informed?

Administrative Support

- What are the administrative responsibilities going to be to implement the staff development and promote professional growth?
- Who is going to actually set up the staff development?

Assessment

- What assessments will be needed to document and measure the development and growth of the staff?
- Does the data support the proposal?
- Will this impact the state test objectives and national standards?
- What data will be required for the assessment of the proposal?

Student Practices and Products

- What will the students be doing differently as a result of the training?
- How will student performance, practices, and products be impacted by the staff development and professional growth?

Curriculum Development

- Will the curriculum require any changes due to the staff development and professional growth?
- Do the current curriculums support the staff development and professional growth?
- Will the changes be departmental or interdisciplinary?

Master Schedule

- Will the master schedule support the staff development?
- What changes in the master schedule might be needed to support the new skills that result from the staff development and professional growth?

Administrative Support

Questions to help begin the discussion, investigation, and consideration of new proposals for administrative support might include:

What administrative support will be required with this action?

- Will administrative support change as a result of this action?
- Will the needed administrative support be available for this action?

What will be the roles of the administrative team with this action?

- Assistant principals, deans, guidance counselors, resource officers
- Secretaries, paraprofessionals, ISS supervisors
- Custodial staff, cafeteria staff

School Board

- Will the school board be involved in this action?
- Are there policies and procedures to be considered?

Facilities

- Will the current facilities and infrastructure support the proposed action?

Site-Based Management

- Is there a decision-making process in place to ensure the staff is involved in making decisions when appropriate?
- Who represents staff to the administrative team (department chairs, team leaders)?

How is the building organized into professional learning communities?

- How does the administrative team support the professional learning communities?
- Do the members of the administrative team make up a PLC?
- Who will be responsible for ensuring the required administrative support is provided?

Staff Development and Professional Growth
Potential Impact on Other SPMS to be Considered

Classroom Instruction

- Does the administrative support proposal affect classroom instruction?

- How will classroom instruction be impacted by the administrative support?

Parent and Community Involvement

- What administrative support will be required to ensure community support?

Staff Development and Professional Growth

- What are the administrative responsibilities necessary to implement the staff development and promote professional growth?

Assessment

- What assessments will be needed to gauge the effectiveness of the administrative support?
- Does the data support the proposal?

Student Practices and Products

- What will the students be doing differently as a result of the administrative action?
- How will student performance, practices, and products be impacted by the administrative action?

Curriculum Development

- Will the changes proposed impact curriculum development?
- Will the changes be departmental or interdisciplinary?

Master Schedule

- Will the master schedule support the changes being considered?
- What changes in the master schedule might be needed to support the changes being considered, and can the administrative team support the changes?

Assessment

Starter questions to help begin the discussion, investigation, and consideration of new proposals for Assessment:

Does the data support the action being considered?

How will the proposed assessments be developed and administered?

- What measurements will be used? (All of the other areas need to be considered for assessment.)
- What will the timelines be?

- How will assessments be reported?
- What changes might we consider depending on what assessments indicate? Who will be responsible for creating the rubrics for each assessment?

How will the action's effect on other areas be assessed?

How will the state test objectives and national standards be affected by this action?

How will the action affect current assessment practices?

- Will changes in current assessment practices be needed with this action?

> **Assessment**
> **Potential Impact on Other SPMS to be Considered**

Classroom Instruction

- What assessments will be required to measure the impact on classroom instruction?
- How will classroom instruction be impacted by the assessments?

Parent and Community Involvement

- What assessments will be required to measure parent and community involvement?

Staff Development and Professional Growth

- How will staff development and professional growth be measured?

Administrative Support

- What assessments will be needed to gauge the effectiveness of the administrative support?
- How will the state test objectives and national standards be affected by the assessment proposal?

Student Practices and Products

- What will the students be doing differently as a result of the assessments?
- How will student performances, practices, and products be impacted by the process?

Curriculum Development

- How will the assessment process impact curriculum development?
- Will the changes be departmental or interdisciplinary?

Master Schedule

- Will the master schedule support the assessment changes being considered?
- What changes in the master schedule might be needed to support the assessment changes being considered?

Student Practices and Products

Questions to help begin the discussion, investigation, and consideration of new proposals for student practices and products might include:

What will the students be "doing" as a result of this action?

- Will the student practices in the classroom change?
- Will the student practices outside of the classroom change?

What will students produce as a result of this action?

- What student products will evidence the new practices?

State test objectives and national standards

- How will the proposed student practices and products affect the state test objectives and national standards?

Who will be responsible for creating the practices and products as a result of this action?

- How will the students be introduced to the new practices they will be performing and products they will be generating?
- What required rubrics for assessing student performance will be needed with each new student practice and product?

Student Practices and Products
Potential Impact on Other SPMS to be Considered

Classroom Instruction

- How will classroom instruction change as a result of the proposal for student practices and products?
- What will the teachers need to implement the new student practices and products?
- Will the teachers need to collaborate across content areas?

Parent and Community Involvement

- How will parent and community involvement be impacted by the proposed student practices and products?

Staff Development and Professional Growth

- What staff development and professional growth will be needed to ensure the proposed student practices and products?

Administrative Support

- What administrative support will be required for the student practices and products?

Assessment

- Will new rubrics need to be developed for the student practices and products?
- How will the student practices and products be assessed in regards to the state standards?

Curriculum Development

- Will curriculum changes be required?
- Will the changes be departmental or interdisciplinary or both?

Master Schedule

- Will the master schedule support the changes being considered?
- What changes in the master schedule might be needed to support the student practices and products being considered?

Parent and Community Involvement

Questions to help begin the discussion, investigation, and consideration of new proposals for Parent and Community Involvement might include:

Parents

- How will the parents be affected by this action?
- In what ways can the parents support this action?
- How do we create parental support for this action?

Business Partners

- Will our business partners be affected by this action?
- In what ways can the partners support this action?
- How do we create the support of our partners for this action?

Community

- What considerations should be given to the rest of the community?
- In what ways can the community support this action?
- How do we create community support for this action?

Media

- How do we ensure appropriate media coverage for this action?
- Can we provide hard copy with pictures for the press?
- Can we provide video for the television stations?
- Do we want the various media on site, or do we want to take the information to the media?

> **Parent and Community Involvement**
> **Potential Impact on Other SPMS to be Considered**

Classroom Instruction

- Will any content areas be affected by parent and community involvement?
- How will classroom instruction be impacted?

Staff Development

- Will the parent and community involvement proposal require staff training?
- Will the parent and community involvement proposal require any other training?

Administrative Support

- What are the administrative responsibilities going to be to implement the community involvement being considered?

Assessment

- What assessments will be needed to gauge staff and community readiness, and the effectiveness of the parent and community involvement being considered?
- Will this impact the state test objectives and national standards?
- Does the data support the parent and community involvement proposal?
- Will this action need to be noted on any of the school reports?

Student Practices and Products

- What will the students be doing differently as a result of the changes?
- How will student performance, practices, and products be impacted by the parent and community involvement?

Curriculum Development

- Will the parent and community involvement proposal require any curriculum changes?

- Will the changes be departmental or interdisciplinary?

Master Schedule

- Will the master schedule support the parent and community involvement?
- What changes might be needed in the master schedule to support the parent and community involvement?

Master Schedule

Questions to help begin the discussion, investigation, and consideration of new proposals for the Master Schedule:

Class Offerings

- Does the proposed action require additional class offerings?
- Does the proposed action require modification of current class offerings?
- What procedures must be followed to make the necessary class offering modifications?

Student Movement

- How will student movement be affected by the proposed change?
- Are there options available to more effectively and efficiently move students?
- How will class placement, locker placements, exploratory class assignments, lunchtimes affect student movement?

Time Distribution

- Does the length of our classes support appropriate instruction?
- How much time should be allotted to passing times, lunch, and advisory?

Small Communities for Learning

- Are the small communities for learning in the best proximity?
- Is there an appropriate place for the teachers assigned to small communities for learning to meet with the appropriate materials available?
- Who is going to be responsible for assessing, building, and modifying the master schedule?

Professional Learning Communities

- Is time built into the day for PLCs to meet?
- Is there a place for the PLCs to meet with the appropriate materials available?

> **Master Schedule**
> **Potential Impact on Other SPMS to be Considered**

Student Practices and Products

- How will student practices and products change as a result of the changes in the master schedule?

Community Involvement

- How will the community be impacted by the proposed changes in the master schedule?

Staff Development and Professional Growth

- What staff development and professional growth will be needed to implement the proposed changes in the master schedule?

Administrative Support

- What administrative support will be required for the changes in the master schedule?

Assessment

- How will the readiness and then the effectiveness of the proposed changes in the master schedule be measured?
- How will the changes be assessed in regards to the state standards?

Curriculum Development

- Will any curriculum areas be affected by the proposed changes in the master schedule?
- Will the changes be departmental or interdisciplinary or both?

Classroom Instruction

- How will the proposed changes in the master schedule impact classroom instruction?

Planning for Programs That Do Not Fit Into Any One School Performance Management System

Some programs do not fit nicely into any one of the school performance management systems. However, the administrative team will still need to consider the impact on all eight of the SPMS that any program might have. For example, advisory programs fit partly into several of the SPMS. There will be a curriculum development component to determine what activities and materials will be needed. There will be a classroom instructional component as the teachers will have advisory groups in their classrooms, and the advisory program will have to be built into the master schedule. In addition to being a part of several of the school systems, the advisory program will certainly impact all of the other systems as well, and should be planned for accordingly.

Administrators will have the opportunity to plan for programs such as advisory in exercise four of the "Tag . . . You're It!" section later. Leaders should create a notebook for keeping up with the changes and impacts that programs will have on the school performance management systems in their building. Simply get a three-ring binder notebook and put the words *Advisory Program* on the outside. Then create full pages of the sample planning forms on pages 54–57 for the advisory planning group to use and keep in the advisory planning notebook. (Of course, depending on the program, you may need multiple copies of some of the forms.) Additional guidelines are described as a part of exercise four.

Differentiated Leadership and the School Performance Management Systems

Differentiated leadership requires an understanding of the interdependent nature of the school performance management systems and how the systems are always interacting with one another. The implication for the administrative team is more comprehensive planning and the need to take into consideration all areas when planning for changes. Just as we plan for "leaving no teacher behind" by using the involvement model of change, here we plan for "leaving no system behind."

Notice that this model is built into the recommended planning process. This planning process requires the administrative team to always be interested in the impact of any proposed change on all of the SPMS. Information is constantly being generated and disseminated, and input is gathered to make decisions regarding the school systems regardless of the proposal. Any in-service and all planning are included in the tasks, and any collateral consequences are considered as a part of the implementation process. If leaders will use the school performance management systems along with the involvement model of change, the school will not end up with the unintended consequences that can develop by having too narrow a focus when planning for a change.

TAG . . . You're It!

Considering the Ripple Effect

Exercise One:

See the example of launching a curriculum mapping process in a school as outlined on pages 30 through 33. On page 30, there are many examples of tasks that would have to be done in the curriculum area. On pages 35 and 36, there are examples of tasks in the other school performance management systems that will result as an impact of the proposal in curriculum development. The administrative team should use this example and replicate the process to discuss, investigate, and consider a possible change in one of the SPMS, or to review and reflect on an existing program in one of the school's systems. Use the appropriate form from pages 54–57 for the SPMS for leading questions to direct the discussion and planning.

Exercise Two:

For an upcoming meeting, practice stating and listing the personal responsibilities during the meeting, and then summarizing the PRs at the conclusion of the meeting. Remember that each PR will need a corresponding timeline.

Exercise Three:

The administrative team should discuss and develop, if needed, the groups in the building that would be responsible for each of the school performance management systems. The SPMS might be a way of dividing the school's leadership team. However it is done, the administrative team needs regular input on the status of the systems and any sub-systems.

Exercise Four:

The administrative team should create a notebook for new programs being considered that do not fit into any one of the school performance management systems. These programs can be planned and documented through the implementation process. The administrative team can use any and all of the forms in this chapter. The form on page 53 can be used as a checklist to keep track of the SPMS considerations, the Staff's Levels of Involvement, and the PRs having been assigned. I have put examples of blank forms on pages 54–57 that should be included in each notebook. Each form should be a separate page in the notebook, and you may need additional copies of some forms.

For example, if your school is going to implement an advisory program, the administrative team would want to create an advisory program planning notebook. In the notebook, there could be the checklist form on page 53 followed by one each of the planning forms on pages 54–57. Fill in the blank planning form with the answers to the questions at the top of the form along with any other questions that come up as a part of the brainstorming process. Continue this process for all of the SPMS as they relate to planning for the implementation of an advisory program.

Then the advisory planning group should fill in the rest of the form with all of the tasks that are ging to be required. The target of involvement might be useful for this process. For each task there must also be a timeline for completion of the task. Finally, the personal responsibilities should be listed for each task, and then summarized again at the completion of each form.

Differentiated Leadership Planning Checklist

Using this form guarantees that all SPMS have been considered, the staff's level of involvement is monitored and noted, and the PRs have been listed. Use this form as a cover sheet for planning.

Group and Organizational Responsibilities Personal Responsibilities	**1. CURRICULUM DEVELOPMENT:** Notes: (Determine Direction) Staff's Level of Involvement (Putting Direction into Practice) __Interest __Information __Input __In-Service __Implementation __Integration
Group and Organizational Responsibilities Personal Responsibilities	**2. CLASSROOM INSTRUCTION:** Notes: (Determine Direction) Staff's Level of Involvement (Putting Direction into Practice) __Interest __Information __Input __In-Service __Implementation __Integration
Group and Organizational Responsibilities Personal Responsibilities	**3. STAFF DEVELOPMENT AND PROFESSIONAL GROWTH:** Notes: (Determine Direction) Staff's Level of Involvement (Putting Direction into Practice) __Interest __Information __Input __In-Service __Implementation __Integration
Group and Organizational Responsibilities Personal Responsibilities	**4. ADMINISTRATIVE SUPPORT:** Notes: (Determine Direction) Staff's Level of Involvement (Putting Direction into Practice) __Interest __Information __Input __In-Service __Implementation __Integration
Group and Organizational Responsibilities Personal Responsibilities	**5. ASSESSMENT:** Notes: (Determine Direction) Staff's Level of Involvement (Putting Direction into Practice) __Interest __Information __Input __In-Service __Implementation __Integration
Group and Organizational Responsibilities Personal Responsibilities	**6. STUDENT PRACTICES AND PRODUCTS:** Notes: (Determine Direction) Staff's Level of Involvement (Putting Direction into Practice) __Interest __Information __Input __In-Service __Implementation __Integration
Group and Organizational Responsibilities Personal Responsibilities	**7. PARENT AND COMMUNITY INVOLVEMENT:** Notes: (Determine Direction) Staff's Level of Involvement (Putting Direction into Practice) __Interest __Information __Input __In-Service __Implementation __Integration
Group and Organizational Responsibilities Personal Responsibilities	**8. MASTER SCHEDULE:** Notes: (Determine Direction) Staff's Level of Involvement (Putting Direction into Practice) __Interest __Information __Input __In-Service __Implementation __Integration

CURRICULUM DEVELOPMENT

Questions to help begin the discussion, investigation, and consideration of new proposals for curriculum development might include:

- Departmental

  Will the proposal involve all of the content areas? If not, which content areas will be involved?

  Will the proposal require new books or other materials?

  Will the proposal require a change in pacing guides?

  Will the proposal require realigning any or all of the curriculums?

- Interdisciplinary

  Will the proposal require interdepartmental collaboration?

  What materials might be required for the new proposal?

ACTIONS AND TASKS REQUIRED AND TIMELINES:

Group, Organizational, and Personal Responsibilities:

1.

2.

3.

CLASSROOM INSTRUCTION

Questions to help begin the discussion, investigation, and consideration of new proposals for classroom instruction might include:

- How will classroom instruction be impacted by this action?

  What change in instruction can be expected?

  Will training be required for the change in classroom instruction?

- What will teachers be "doing" in the classroom as a result of this action?

- Who will be responsible for making any needed changes in classroom instruction?

  Who will be responsible for materials, accountability, and training?

- What classroom materials, if any, will be needed? How will classroom instruction be impacted by this action?

ACTIONS AND TASKS REQUIRED AND TIMELINES:

Group, Organizational, and Personal Responsibilities:

1.

2.

3.

STAFF DEVELOPMENT AND PROFESSIONAL GROWTH

Questions to help begin the discussion, investigation, and consideration of new proposals for staff development and professional growth might include:

- What staff development will be required for this proposal?

- What professional growth will there be as a result of this action?

- Professional Learning Communities
  Do our current professional learning communities enable us to train and support the proposed action?

- Do new professional learning communities need to be created to support the proposed action?

- Who will be responsible for organizing the staff development?

ACTIONS AND TASKS REQUIRED AND TIMELINES:

Group, Organizational, and Personal Responsibilities:

1.

2.

3.

ADMINISTRATIVE SUPPORT

Questions to help begin the discussion, investigation, and consideration of new proposals for administrative support might include:

- What administrative support will be required with this action?
  Will administrative support change as a result of this action?
  Will the needed administrative support be available for this action?

- What will the roles of the administrative team be with this action?
  Assistant principals, deans, guidance counselors, resource officers
  Secretaries, paraprofessionals, ISS supervisors
  Custodial staff, cafeteria staff

- School Board
  Will the school board be involved in this action?
  Are there policies and procedures to be considered?

- Facilities
  Will the current facilities and infrastructure support the proposed action?

- Site-Based Management
  Is there a decision-making process in place to ensure the staff is involved in making decisions when appropriate?
  Who represents staff to the administrative team? (department chairs, team leaders)

ACTIONS AND TASKS REQUIRED AND TIMELINES:
Group, Organizational, and Personal Responsibilities:

1.   2.   3.

ASSESSMENT

Questions to help begin the discussion, investigation, and consideration of new proposals for assessment might include:

- Does the data support the action being considered?

- How will the proposed assessments be developed and administered?
  What measurements will be used?

- All of the other areas need to be considered for assessment.
  What will the timelines be?
  How will assessments be reported?
  What changes might we consider depending on what assessments indicate?

- Who will be responsible for creating the rubrics for each assessment?

- How will the action's effects on other areas be assessed?

- State test objectives and national standards
  How will the state test objectives and national standards be affected
    by this action?

- How will the action affect current assessment practices?
  Will changes in current assessment practices be needed with this action?

ACTIONS AND TASKS REQUIRED AND TIMELINES:

Group, Organizational, and Personal Responsibilities:

1.   2.   3.

STUDENT PRACTICES AND PRODUCTS

Questions to help begin the discussion, investigation, and consideration of new proposals for student practices and products might include:

- What will the students be "doing" as a result of this action?
  Will the student practices in the classroom change?
  Will the student practices outside the classroom change?

- What will students produce as a result of this action?
  What student products will evidence the new practices?

- How will the students be introduced to the new practices they will be performing and products they will be generating?

- Rubrics for assessing student performance will be required with each new student practice and products.

- State test objectives and national standards
  How will the proposed student practices and products affect the state
    test objectives and national standards?

ACTIONS AND TASKS REQUIRED AND TIMELINES:

Group, Organizational, and Personal Responsibilities:

1.

2.

3.

Differentiated Leadership
Copyright ©2008 by Incentive Publications, Inc., Nashville, TN.

PARENT AND COMMUNITY INVOLVEMENT

Questions to help begin the discussion, investigation, and consideration of new proposals for parent and community involvement might include:

- Parents
  How will the parents be affected by this action?
  In what ways can the parents support this action?
  How do we create parental support for this action?
- Partners
  Will any of our partners be affected by this action?
  In what ways can the partners support this action?
  How do we create the support of our partners for this action?
- Community
  What considerations should be given to the rest of the community?
  In what ways can the community support this action?
  How do we create community support for this action?
- Media
  How do we ensure appropriate media coverage for this action?
  Can we provide hard copy with pictures for the press?
  Can we provide video for the television stations?
  Do we want the various media on site, or do we want to take the information to the media?

ACTIONS AND TASKS REQUIRED AND TIMELINES:

Group, Organizational, and Personal Responsibilities:

1.   2.   3.

MASTER SCHEDULE

Questions to help begin the discussion, investigation, and consideration of new proposals for the master schedule might include:

- Class Offerings
- Does the proposed action require additional class offerings?
- Does the proposed action require modification of current class offerings?
- What procedures must be followed to make the necessary class offering modifications?
- Student movement
- How will student movement be affected by the proposed change?
  Are there options available to more effectively and efficiently move students? (Class placement, locker placements, exploratory class assignments, lunchtimes)
- Time distribution
- Length of classes
  Does the length of our classes support appropriate instruction?
- Passing times, lunch, advisory
- Who is going to be responsible for assessing, building, and modifying the master schedule?
- Staffing
- Does the proposal require a change in staffing?

ACTIONS AND TASKS REQUIRED AND TIMELINES:

Group, Organizational, and Personal Responsibilities:

1.   2.   3.

Group Dynamics

Leading Productive Groups

I will never forget being called to a group meeting once. My secretary at the time reached me on a walkie-talkie, telling me that my presence was needed in one of the planning rooms right away. Her insistence and the concern I could hear in her voice meant that I should hustle, so I got to the room very quickly. As I entered the room, one of the teachers was throwing a large three-ring binder notebook into the middle of the table which caused papers to fly everywhere.

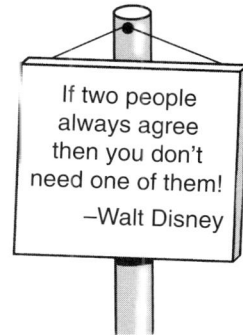

As the notebook landed, she also called another one of the teachers in the room a very uncomplimentary word. The teacher had her back to me as I was entering, and she turned quickly to leave the room and quite literally ran into me. Without missing a beat, she placed her index finger in the middle of my chest with a fair amount of force and all but yelled, "And it's your fault!" I must also say that she put very heavy emphasis on the "your," and then she went on down the hallway. Being the astute and observant administrator that I was, and having been trained in conflict management, I concluded that this group was having a problem. Not only that, at least from one person's perspective, it was apparently my fault. More on this particular situation later . . . .

Differentiated leadership means being able to deal with diverse people working together in a variety of groups assigned with a variety of tasks. So now let's get to work on identifying what happens in groups and what leaders might be able to do about the situations as they arise. Of course, the best thing is for the administrative team to be proactive, which means preparing all of your groups for potential situations before they happen. Even with the best training, many groups will still experience situations that will require leadership interventions. This means that administrators need to understand group dynamics and the developmental phases that all groups will go through.

Group members should be trained to understand and recognize the incremental phases they will have to go through as they proceed from being assigned to a group to becoming a contributing member of a successful working group. Recognizing the various stages of group development will empower administrators and group members to anticipate the issues that are a natural part of group development. With this understanding, leaders and group members can also recognize when situations arise that are out of the ordinary in group development.

After I walk the administrative team through the stages of group development and their characteristics, I will share what to do when group dysfunctions occur. I am going to share several generic situations that leaders might face in dealing with the many groups in their building. Then I will give administrators some potential causes and solutions for the various group situations described. This will help administrators to diagnose problems and have the appropriate prescriptions on hand.

I like to relate the four phases of group development to the phases of human growth that we are all so familiar with. In the book *Get Fit!*, I have an entire chapter dedicated to these phases. I will give you a very brief description here, and refer you to *Get Fit!* for more details. The four phases of group development are: Toddler, Early Adolescent, Adolescent, and Mature. You will also notice that the four phases form the acronym T.E.A.M. When a group has moved through the four developmental phases they become a working team. The word group in this chapter could refer to an academy, a team, a department, a committee, a two-person coteaching team, or an administrative team.

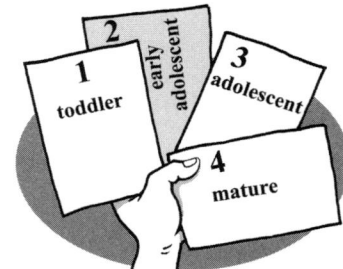

Stage One
Toddler

- Early Childhood
  Coworkers are just beginning to find the group's balance.

- Building Trust
  Groups begin to work through a few issues and members start to build trust.
  Trust-building activities can help at this stage.

- Establishing Purpose and Guiding Principles
  Group members need to develop a common vision of the group's purpose.

- In-Service Is Critical
  Training increases group performance and helps limit anxiety.

- Need for Information
  Feedback is very important.

- Communication skills that determine the quality of information exchange are developing.
  The quality and quantity of information provided can help address confusion.

- Individual Learning
  Group members tend to learn in reference to their personal situation.

- Feelings
  Excitement
  Anxiety
  Confusion

Stage Two
Early Adolescence

- Puberty
  Need I say more?

- Most Difficult Time
  If a group is going to have a rough spot, this is the time. (During the first stage, the members are mostly focused on the process and mechanics of being a group.)

- Deal with Personalities
  The group members are learning how to deal with and accommodate each group member's individual style and personality.
  Competition can occur between group members.

- Mastering the Mechanics
  The group should be better at running meetings and should be more efficient with time management.

- In-Service Needed
  Follow-up training should focus on conflict management and group function as well as group product. (Members will share more, but still learn independently.)

- Feelings
  Accomplishment and connectedness
  Stress and frustration

Stage Three
Adolescent

- High Level of Collaboration
  Group members have worked through power issues.
  Roles and responsibilities for the team are freely shared
  among the team members.

- Consensus Is More Easily Achieved.
  Group members have learned about each other's priorities
  and make accommodations for each other.

- Group Members Empower Each Other.
  Team members have learned how to agree to disagree,
  move on, and still back each other.

- Group Learning
  Group members are beginning to see training
  through the eyes of the group as well as individually.

- In-Service Needed
  Any additional training should focus on group product.

- Little or No Competition
  Group members have learned that success for any member
  is success for the entire group.

- Feelings
  Control and support
  Empowerment and confidence

Stage Four
Mature

- Adult Stage
  Group members feel more in control.
  The group members now feel like the group is working for
  them, instead of their working for the group.

- Group Members Are in Alignment.
  A high level of trust has been established,
  and a common language has emerged.
  The mechanics of meetings are second nature.
  The group can take on tasks which are much more complex.

- Consensus Is Easily Achieved.
  Group members have learned about each other's priorities and make accommodations for each other.
  The group handles politics in a straightforward manner.

- In-Service Needed
  Any additional training should be group driven.

- Roles and Responsibilities Are Shared Freely by All Team Members.

- The Group Members Take Responsibility for Each Other.
  Group members are confident in representing, and being represented by, each other.

- Feelings
  Collaboration and freedom
  Control and confidence

Group Dynamics

Here are a few situations that leaders face when working with people in groups. All groups will have issues to resolve in order to keep the group viable and productive. The purpose of this section is diagnostic, and then prescriptive for the administrative team. Read about the issue that may occur in groups, a possible reason for the issue, and a solution for administrators to consider when dealing with the situation. *(In the last situation, you will also see what happened with my opening story.)*

The Issue:

The group never seems to come to conclusion with topics.

The Reason:

The group likes to explore all of the possibilities and has difficulty coming to closure on topics.

The Solution:

The group needs training and practice with setting rigid time limits for topics. Get a timer (I like the wind-up timers) and establish a time limit for each aspect of the meeting. In the chapter on differentiated staff meetings, I talk about assigning "periods" or time limits to each topic. One "period" is five minutes. The group should preassign an appropriate number of periods to each area of discussion. Then, as the time is expiring, the group should be prodded to decide on an action and come to closure. Assign a group member as the timekeeper to remind the group of time remaining and help move the group to closure. An administrator may need to remind and encourage the group to move from discussion to action.

The Issue:

The same people seem to be doing the majority of the work for the group. When there are follow-up tasks as a result of the group meetings, the workload is not evenly distributed.

The Reason:

Some people in groups really think they are doing more for the group than they actually are, so they do not understand that they are not carrying their part of the workload. Some people volunteer for every job and want to be the ones doing the bulk of the work for the group. Some people simply will not take on extra work unless asked, and in some groups, there are people that are not willing to ask. They would simply rather do it themselves. These situations can cause frustration and bad feelings if allowed to go on for any length of time.

The Solution:

Often, there are actions that are implied during meetings, but the meeting is allowed to end without someone stating who was supposed to do the tasks. The group needs to be reminded to assign personal responsibilities (PRs) for each task that might come up during a meeting. With every topic, the recorder or some other group member needs to ask the group, "Who is going to be personally responsible for this action?" This should happen every time there is an implied action or task during a discussion. In addition to asking about the PRs during the meeting, no meeting should ever end without the recorder reviewing the personal responsibilities (PRs) that resulted from that meeting. If there were no PRs for the meeting, that should be stated at the closure of the meeting. So every meeting should end with the statement, "The PRs for this meeting are as follows . . . ."

The administrative team should request that the PRs also be stated cumulatively, at least monthly, as a part of the group's regular self-assessment. When the PRs are stated, published, and shared often, it becomes very clear to everyone if the responsibilities for the group are being evenly distributed. Part of the training for working in a group would be the need for self-assessment, and everyone in the group should know that this is going to be a part of the group function. Should an administrator need to become involved to help motivate a group member, he or she will have the documentation of the group member's lack of contributions to the group's tasks.

The Issue:

The group has trouble getting started, and then has trouble staying on task during meetings.

The Reason:

The group members arrive late for the meetings and are often unprepared. The group members often start side conversations that get the group off task. The group members do not know what the topics are for the meeting, and decide on discussion topics on the fly causing the meetings to wander.

The Solution:

Agendas! Many groups do not like to have set agendas, but without the structure of an agenda the meeting will wander. The agenda for the meeting, with the topics and the number of periods for each topic, should be established prior to the meeting. If the members of the group know that the first few minutes of the meeting will be deciding what to talk about, they will be more likely to be late. If the meetings start on time with the topics already known to the participants, the group members are much more likely to be on time.

The group members need to know what the topics are going to be if they are to be expected to be prepared for the meetings. For example, in the case of academies or teams, if they set Tuesdays for discipline referral reviews, everyone knows to bring their referrals to the meetings on Tuesdays. Also, this helps the administrator who will be a part of the discipline reviews know when to attend these meetings. (Discipline reviews are discussed in the chapter on student management.)

The Issue:

There appear to be personality conflicts within the group. Some group members have shared they are not getting along with other members of the group.

The Reason:

Members of the group sound accusatory or judgmental to other members of the group. Group members get defensive during meetings.

The Solution:

The administrative team will need to work with the group to get them to focus on the tasks and the mechanics of the group. The more mechanical the functions are, the less opportunity there will be for personal issues to be a part of the conversation. The group will also need to be reminded to state difficulties in relation to the issues and not to any person in the group. Of course, group members will also have to be reminded not to attach themselves to issues. That way, the person that proposed the field trip should not take it personally if members of the group state reasons that might conflict with the proposed field trip.

Continued training should focus on the language of the group, reminding them not to use words like "you," "always," "never," or any type of negative stereotyping. This is also very common for newer groups, and less common as groups continue to work together.

The Issue:

The discussion of topics lacks focus. The group appears to be disorganized. There is no record of meetings to review, and so on.

The Reason:

The group does not have assigned roles and responsibilities.

The Solution:

(Okay, you knew this was coming.) Assign roles and responsibilities to every group member. Some of the roles that need to be

assigned for every group are: leader, facilitator, recorder, timekeeper, communicator, materials person, and so on. A brief description of the roles with the responsibilities for each role is listed below. For some groups, there may be the need for additional roles depending in the purpose of the group; but the roles and responsibilities listed here are important for the mechanics of any group.

The Issue:

There is little enthusiasm. The group seems to lack motivation.

The Reason:

There is no clear understanding of the group purpose. The group has no benchmarks to indicate progress, so the group does not know how much they have accomplished.

The Solution:

The group needs to reestablish its purpose and define clear and measurable goals. The group needs to establish timelines with measurable benchmarks. The group will then have to have designated meetings for assessing their progress. The group should establish both cognitive goals for progress and affective goals for function. The group should also plan celebrations for accomplishing preestablished benchmarks and achieving goals.

The Issue:

There seems to be confusion about intent. Group members come away from the meeting with different understandings. This often is demonstrated in future meetings with statements indicating confusion like, "Oh, I thought we had decided something else."

The Problem:

The communicators are not checking for understanding, and the group members are not always actively engaged in discussions.

The Solution:

The administrative team will want to periodically review active listening techniques with the group. Remind the members about eye contact, body lean, and other nonverbal indicators of active engagement with the speaker. Group members should paraphrase often and ask questions for clarification. This is often a problem in newer groups. As groups are together longer, the group members begin to understand "how" each member obtains his or her information. Members will become more skilled in reading each other's nonverbal clues and will be more willing to check for understanding.

The Issue:

The group is in a highly agitated state, and emotions are running high. *(Remember the first situation I described at the beginning of this chapter? This definitely describes their situation.)*

The Problem:

The group is unable to reach consensus because of deep-seated beliefs or concerns of members that differ from each other.

I know that many administrators will laugh and completely understand when I share that the topic of discussion that lead to the notebook throwing and name calling was that topic of consternation: gum chewing!

The group I was referring to earlier was an interdisciplinary team of teachers. I had charged all of the teams to come up with common policies that would be the same as students moved from class to class on their team. That would include things like paper headings, homework grading policies, extra-credit policies, and so on. We did not have a schoolwide gum chewing policy, and this particular group was trying to decide whether they were going to let the students on their team chew gum.

The Solution:

It is all right to agree to disagree in some instances. The group needs to be reminded, and in my case, be given a little extra

Differentiated Leadership
Copyright ©2008 by Incentive Publications, Inc., Nashville, TN.

coaching, about how to agree to disagree. The key is to still back each other up, and in the example case, to let the students know that the entire team was in on the decision as to where the students could and could not chew gum.

As we worked through the issue, the team decided that everyone but the science teacher would allow students to chew gum. But they would not say things like "Mr. Jones does not allow gum chewing." Instead, they would indicate that as a team, all the teachers together had made the decision that gum chewing would be allowed in all classes except science. In this case, they told the students it was because of the occasional use of lab equipment and so on.

Now here is how to agree to disagree. The science teacher agreed not to handle gum chewing as a disciplinary issue in his class. Since the students were allowed to chew gum in their other classes, the team knew that the students would occasionally forget and continue chewing their gum in science class. Every teacher reminds the students at the end of each period, that if they are going to science, to get rid of their gum. The science teacher reminds the students at the beginning of each period and, if he sees gum, he simply tells the students to get rid of it.

A group can agree to disagree, but they also have to talk through the situations that might occur due to this agreement and make accommodations accordingly for each other. And as Paul Harvey would say, "Now you know the rest of the story!"

Conclusion

Administrators have to deal with different groups all the time, and differentiated leadership means working to understand group dynamics. Every group develops its own personality which becomes a blend of the individual personalities that make up the group members. All group members are not always going to get along all of the time, and in fact, it is in the tension created by members challenging each other that the greatest growth can occur. Of course, the trick is getting the group members to challenge each other in ways that do not promote defensiveness. When group members get defensive, they cannot listen very well.

Differentiated leadership implies that the leaders are very actively engaged with the groups as well as the individuals in the school. Once groups have been implemented, administrators (remembering the involvement model of change) need to have ways to maintain the interest level, get input from those groups, and provide information and additional training as needed. To get regular input, I created a TLC, which means exactly what you might guess—tender, loving care. My TLC was made up of all of the group leaders in my building. At the high school, that included all of the departments and academies, as well as any other committees or groups, including parent or business groups. In the middle school, the TLC would also include interdisciplinary teams, if teams are a part of your program.

The expectation was that all group leaders would give input about the operation of their groups. Of course, each group had a member of the administrative team that was assigned to it. The administrative team would meet once a week, and the TLC would meet every other week, so that regular input about the functioning of the various groups was given and received in a variety of ways. Notice that the personal responsibilities (PRs) and timelines are clear. This gives the administrative team several ways to gauge the interest level of the groups, disseminate and receive information, and use the input to support the groups as they implement their responsibilities. Differentiated leadership is about building systems where the involvement model of change is almost self-sustaining.

TAG . . . You're It!

Take Time to Think About Groups

Exercise One:

The administrative team should make a list of the various groups in the building. Then discuss and try to come to consensus as to what stage of development each group is in. As an administrative team, discuss what supports would be most appropriate for each group at their particular stage of development.

Exercise Two:

The administrative team should review the group dynamic examples above and share experiences members have had and how they were resolved. Then discuss whether similar issues are currently occurring within groups in the school, and if so, how they might be best resolved.

Student Management

Interactive Student Management Strategies

Most administrative teams will agree that an inordinate amount of their time is taken up with student management issues. Student management issues usually dominate the interaction between the administrators and the staff. The focus of this chapter is to help administrators work with the staff to collaborate efficiently and effectively when dealing with disciplinary issues. Successful leaders have developed a culture where discipline is equally everyone's responsibility.

> Every disciplinary issue should be a learning opportunity.

Some staff members are more skilled at student management than others. Every staff member has his or her own "style" for handling student management in the classroom. The question for the administrative team is how do you teach and coach diverse styles and get everyone to continue to improve their student management skills. The key is to create systems that enable staff collaboration. Every disciplinary issue should be a learning opportunity, and of course, here is where differentiated leadership comes in.

In this chapter, I will present ways for administrators and teachers to become more proactive with student management. First, I will show how teachers and administrators can identify discipline issues and then share student management strategies for the issues at hand. Then I am going to explain how to dramatically reduce the time and energy administrators and teachers spend on discipline by heading off inappropriate student behaviors before they get serious enough to become referrals.

Can We Talk? Discipline Referral Reviews

Administrative teams need to have a way of getting the staff invested in each other's discipline. Every teacher is interested in his or her own students. Therefore, the way to do this is to have a system for the staff to share student management information with each other. Teachers want, and need, to know if their students are having discipline issues. The trick is to build into the system a way for the teachers to receive input from each other. This is the only way the teachers cumulatively and individually can make the best decisions regarding any student management issue. Notice that this discipline system follows the involvement model of change. The administrative team will have to get the teachers interested to get them to share information and receive input from each other in order to make quality decisions.

If your school has academies or teams, this process works best as a part of academy or team meetings. In lieu of academies or teams, some schools have success using each of the planning periods during the day to bring together the teachers. *(As a high school assistant principal, I would ask the teachers to meet with me once every two weeks for the first 20 minutes of their planning time on Thursdays. As I did the discipline referral review process, these teachers may or may not have all of the students in the review, but they all have to deal with similar situations in their classrooms as those on the referrals.)*

The administrator brings all of the referrals written by those teachers who are in attendance since the last referral review meeting to each referral review meeting. The administrator simply reads the first referral to the teachers and shares what he or she did in response to the referral. Then the teachers and the administrator discuss and make suggestions to aid with future situations like the one described. The administrator will ask leading questions such as, "What would you have done in that situation? Is there any way to deal with the situation rather than to make a referral? Did I deal with the referral in a way that was satisfactory to you? Would you suggest any changes in the wording for the referral?" The teachers should not spend a great deal of time on each referral and should try to come to consensus quickly and move on to the next referral. Several things happen as a result of these discipline referral reviews.

Reviewing disciplinary referrals is the best way for teachers and administrators to share information and specific strategies for dealing with discipline. Each review is a chance to study referrals, and is also the best way to "norm" the referral process. The teachers need to be consistent in identifying types of behaviors that result in a referral, and in the wording that describes those behaviors. The administrators need to be consistent in the way they deal with types of referrals the team is going to send them. *(Sometimes administrators I have worked with complain about the inconsistency of the referrals they receive, and on occasion the teachers complain about the inconsistencies of the administrators dealing with the referrals. This process eliminates all of these issues and provides a quick way to get everyone on the same page.)*

This is absolutely the only way I have found to norm the referral process. It is very powerful for teachers to know that when they write referrals, the referrals will eventually be read to their colleagues in a

Differentiated Leadership
Copyright ©2008 by Incentive Publications, Inc., Nashville, TN.

review process. So the teachers get to see if other teachers are writing students up for not bringing pencils *(I have had this happen),* and to see how the other teachers deal with situations. The administrators know that they will face the teachers after dealing with each referral. The administrator and the teachers need the feedback from the team regarding how the referral was dealt with if the referral process is going to continually improve. Some teachers have been known to share their thoughts about how discipline is being handled in the teachers' lounge. The disciplinary referral studies help clear up any misunderstandings, and will help each side of the referral process better understand the other.

Differentiated leadership is about helping all staff members learn and grow, which is what happens when the groups the administrative team works with actually become professional learning communities. I called my high-school planning period meetings "Professional Learning Communities for the Review of Discipline Procedures," and we included these meetings as a part of our school improvement plan. There is a longitudinal study built right into the process in that the teachers are going to hear and discuss referrals all year, and will be able to study which strategies work and which ones do not. To carry this process one step further, some schools have groups that have discipline strategy study sessions.

Discipline Strategy Study Sessions

The entire purpose of a "Student Management Study Group" is to discuss, investigate, and consider what options are available to the staff when dealing with student management issues. Student management study groups can use the form on page 92 for listing disciplinary strategies. Notice there are three specific uses for the form. Fill in the person or the group that will use the strategies in the blank. One form should list "frontline" disciplinary intervention strategies used by individual teachers in the classroom. If your school has academies or teams, another form should list strategies that can be used by those academies or teams. The last form is a list of strategies that might be available to the school.

The individual teacher intervention strategies list might start out with such things as proximity, change in student seating, talking to a student in the hallway, calling parents, and discipline referral. The academy or team strategies list might start out with such things as bringing a student into an academy or team meeting to meet with the group of teachers, referring the student to the counselor, assigning an academy or team detention, and having a conference with the parents. The school strategies list usually contains interventions by administrators and counselors and might start with such things as meeting with a counselor, before- or after-school detentions, in-school suspension, and out-of-school suspension. The lists should be as comprehensive as possible, covering subtle strategies to the most direct interventions.

Notice the form has two parts. First, there is a place on the form for indicating and documenting the strategies that are available to help specific students. The teachers use the first part of the form as a reference list. The second part is for listing the strategies that have actually been used, with the date and time the strategy was used.

Again, the idea is for administrators and the student management study group to make available a menu of options for the teachers that can also serve as a checklist for easy documentation of interventions that have been attempted. It will be helpful to have these lists available for the discipline referral review meetings.

*N*ow I want to share the most interactive, proactive student management program that I have come across. This next process may be the definition of differentiated leadership in the way that this process enables leaders to bring together all staff members to collaborate on positive reinforcements with proactive student management strategies and consequences.

Reactive Student Management Systems

Administrative teams know that most student management procedures are reactive in structure. That is, a series of consequences are established to deal with the anticipated, inappropriate student behaviors. When a student acts inappropriately, the teacher reacts with the appropriate consequence. If the inappropriate behavior persists, the teacher will react with the next level of consequence. This will go on until the behaviors and consequences get serious enough to call for administrative interventions. An administrator will then react to what the teacher sends in the way of a referral, and he or she will begin to impose another incremental series of consequences.

This system operates on the premise that the student will eventually "learn" from the one or more of the consequences not only what behaviors were inappropriate, but also what the appropriate behaviors are, and will make the personal adjustments as needed. This system is essential, and in most schools is actually implemented to a pretty high level. Yet, most schools still seem to have enough discipline issues to keep the administrative team busy and, in many cases, overwhelmed. That is because this system of "reactions" and "consequences" is only one-third of the battle. Schools that also implement a system of proactive student management interventions along with a system of positive reinforcements create a balance that results in far fewer discipline referrals.

Positive Reinforcements and Proactive Student Management

In this system, administrators combine proactive student management strategies with positive reinforcements for appropriate behaviors. Schools that have systems of positive reinforcements for the students do not have the quantity of student management issues that other schools do. The idea is to show the students how to stay out of trouble before they get into trouble, whether it is with academic or disciplinary issues. This system also enables administrators and counselors to become involved with students well before the referral process, which in most cases precludes the eventual need for referrals at all. This process is also discussed in detail in *Get Fit!* from the teacher's perspective. You will see that this process almost requires the "small communities for learning" of academies or teams.

Let's Give a Thumbs Up for Student Success!

This process requires the administrative team, in which I include counselors, to meet with teachers in groups to discuss students. In smaller schools, this can be accomplished with grade-level meetings. In midsized and larger schools, there will need to be smaller groups of teachers that can meet to discuss the students they teach. So this process pretty much requires schools to have interdisciplinary academies or teams which, of course, break the students into smaller groups. This way the administrative team can meet with an academy or team and deal with all of their students, and then work with the next academy or team until all of the students in the building have been discussed.

Therefore, for the rest of this chapter, I am going to handle the use of teams and academies as I do in other sections of this book. I will use the term "team" in all of its forms to also refer to an "academy." The system I am referring to is run by a series of team meetings that are called Thumbs Meetings. Administrators will like how this system focuses on the positive—beginning with its name and running throughout the process. Administrators are stretched beyond belief and will appreciate that the beauty of this system is in its simplicity.

Leaders that work with teams know that it is very rare that a team is able to bring up every single student on the team by name during any one team meeting, or even over a period of several team meetings. And the administrators can tell you which students are the ones being discussed during team meetings. During Thumbs Meetings, every individual student is mentioned by name, and the group of teachers, administrator, and counselor will determine what recognition or intervention would be most appropriate for that student.

The first thing administrators will be thinking is "that will be a lot of students to discuss in a fairly short period of time," and they are absolutely correct. In a moment, you will see that the way the administrative team runs these meetings makes this not only possible, but actually pretty simple. Most administrative teams have the interdisciplinary teams run these meetings every two weeks. By having teams run these meetings every other week, administrators can go to half of the Thumbs Meetings on the even weeks, and the other half of the Thumbs Meetings on the odd weeks. The administrative team will divide up the interdisciplinary teams between them so that even in very large schools, administrators do not have to attend more than two or three of these Thumbs meetings in a week. This will make it easier for the administrative team to ensure that an administrator will be at every Thumbs Meeting. It is critical that a counselor also attend these meetings.

Thumbs Meetings are successful because it is absolutely, positively vital and nonnegotiable that an administrator and a counselor attend this team meeting. The administrator and counselor will lead the team in a discussion about each student on the team individually, in five criteria areas. As a result of these Thumbs Meetings, every student on the team will receive some feedback about their performance. The administrative team will know at the conclusion of each meeting who is personally responsible for providing the feedback and interventions as a part of the follow-through of the Thumbs Meetings.

Most schools like to provide some written form of feedback to the students as a result of the Thumbs Meetings. In that case, every two weeks each student will receive a certificate

recognizing their efforts, or a notice of the need for them to improve their behavior or their academic efforts. And yes, sometimes students may need to improve their efforts in both areas. Several of the schools I work with like to use the name "Thumbs Up Certificate" for the recognition, and "Heads Up Notice" for the needs improvement notice. It has been my experience that even in difficult schools, based on the criteria and the way the system works, most students will eventually begin to receive recognition for their efforts. Administrators will appreciate that every student will also write a goal statement every two weeks.

The administrative team will need to demonstrate this process. There is no question it will take a little practice as everyone gets the timing down. It happens quite frequently that some students will actually receive both recognition and some sort of intervention. This system ensures that no students are overlooked for intervention consideration. *(You will see a lot of "gray area" students getting more support.)* The leaders will share with teachers how the recognition and the interventions are based on the five criteria that the teachers consider as they go through the names of the students on the team.

The Mechanics of a Fine-tuned Program

To demonstrate how the system works, the administrative team will need a roster of the students they will be working with. If your school has an advisory program, you will want to use the advisory class lists. In lieu of an advisory program, the leaders might encourage the interdisciplinary team to consider using either their first- or last-period class list. Remember that the teachers will be giving students certificates and having them fill out goal sheets. Therefore, the teachers will want to select a period that lends itself best to taking a few minutes every couple of weeks for this process. The mechanics of the meeting are quite simple.

If your school has an advisory program, this process should become a part of the advisory program. The teacher will be a real advisor as he or she processes the Thumbs Meetings with his or her students. However, this process can also happen in the last few minutes of one of the other classes ever two weeks. Some schools like to do this in last period just before the students leave, and others prefer just before lunch. In both instances, students are sometimes less than focused on the regular curriculum.

For management purposes, it is handy to have two copies of the class lists. Someone will read the names off one list while someone else is making notes on the other list. Of course, those two people should be the counselor and the administrator that are in attendance. The administrator or counselor reads the names of each of the students on the team, and as each name is read, the team members quite literally indicate either a thumbs up or a thumbs down with their hands. *(Think gladiators!)* If the administrator is reading the names, the counselor will be the recorder and will record which teachers indicate a thumbs down for each student.

Administrators, here is another important management issue. There is to be absolutely no talking allowed during the first phase of the meeting. This is the phase where the names are being read and the teachers are only indicating a thumbs up or a thumbs down for each name. The only person that is allowed to talk is the person reading the names, and that person only pauses very briefly for the recorder to see how many thumbs-down signals there are for each name, and mark it accordingly. You will have to remind teachers from time to time that no discussion is allowed during this part of the meeting; each teacher only indicates a thumbs up or a thumbs down for each student as each name is read. This is why the team is able to get through a lot of names very quickly.

With no discussion, the reading of the names with the indicating and recording of a thumbs-up signal or thumbs-down signal will develop into a rhythm that will pace the meeting. A thumbs-up signal indicates that teacher feels the student is currently being successful in each of the five areas. A team member indicates a concern in any one or more areas by showing a thumbs-down signal as a student's name is read. Any thumbs-down signal will require discussion at the end of the first phase, and some intervention will be assigned.

The five criteria that I recommend administrative teams suggest teachers consider are: academic effort, behavior, social, emotional, and personal issues. For the academic area, that question is whether or not the student is giving each teacher his or her best effort in class. Administrators will want to make the distinction that this is not grade based. The academic concern for the Thumbs Up system is based on the student's efforts in each of the teacher's classes, and not on academic ability. Therefore if a student is trying in a class, that would merit a thumbs up regardless of the grade associated with those efforts. Teachers are very accustomed to grade-based systems, and I have found that I have to continually coach them in this area early in the process. You will also see that for this process to work, teachers should always err on the side of the positive. Any time at all that a student demonstrates any improvement at all from previous effort, the student should earn a thumbs up from a teacher.

Teachers are not used to indicating that they are having any student management issues until those issues have reached the referral stage. For this process to work, administrators will want to work with the teachers to understand that for disciplinary issues, the teachers should indicate a thumbs down if the student is causing any student management issues at all. In other words, if the student is even in the beginning stages of any disciplinary procedures for a teacher, then that teacher should indicate thumbs down. For administrators to be proactive with student management, they need to know when students are just beginning to cause problems. Administrators need information to know what and where those problems are if they are to intervene prior to the referral stage.

Most administrative teams include social, emotional, and personal concerns as part of the criteria for teachers to consider as this enables the counselor to also be proactive with students. Administrators will want teachers to consider if each student is fitting in with his or her peer group as well as might be expected. Being a loner is not a bad thing; however, being a loner because the other students do not want to have anything to do with the student is not a healthy thing. School leaders know that this is a student who would benefit from a good counselor's help. Students at this age are naturally emotional, but occasionally they are even a little more emotional than is typical for this age. This, along with any personal issues like poor hygiene, would be something to make the counselor aware of. So, as a part of this process, administrators would request that any teacher who has a concern about social, emotional, or personal issues for a particular student indicate thumbs down when that student's name was read.

Remember, this process is for both positive reinforcement and for interventions. Administrators will need to make one point very clear. It is very important that everyone know and understand that the social, emotional, and personal concerns are never part of the consideration for whether or not a student will receive recognition. These criteria are included as a part of the discussion because it is critical to provide support for students experiencing difficulties in these areas. Only disciplinary needs and academic effort will be considered for whether or not a student will receive recognition.

For example: a student might be performing very well, but might receive one or more thumbs-down signals from teachers due to social, emotional, or personal concerns. This student would absolutely receive the positive recognition for the academic effort and behavior! But the administrator would lead the discussion with the team and the counselor about what support, such as peer mentoring or counseling, might be appropriate for this student as he or she works through these issues.

After going through all of the names of all of the students on the team, the administrator or counselor will read back the names of the students receiving any thumbs down from any of the teachers. The administrator and counselor will review with the team these students that have received one or more thumbs-down signals. Then the group will decide on the best course of action for each student. As you will see, there are several appropriate follow-up interventions available depending on the areas of concern. Everyone will leave the meeting knowing who is personally responsible for what interventions, and for which students.

Administrators know that for interventions to be helpful, they must be timely. Therefore, the administrators will want to encourage everyone to begin following up with their students immediately after the meeting. The day immediately following the Thumbs Meeting, the teachers will follow up with their students by giving out the various certificates to the students. They will give out "Thumbs-Up" certificates that will recognize those students giving their best efforts, and the "Heads-Up" notices for those students who are not performing up to the teacher's expectations. Immediately after the Thumbs Meeting, the administrator and the counselor will begin follow-up interventions for students needing their assistance. I will share the administrative and counseling interventions a little later.

By far, the greatest number of students will merit recognition. Most of the schools that use this system have a recognition committee, or the teams themselves, to come up with some sort of "Thumbs-Up" award to give out to students who are demonstrating academic effort and behaving in their classes. The certificate may or may not actually say anything about thumbs up, but should recognize the student's efforts. Sample certificates for recognition and notices for improvement that teams around the country have used can be found in the book *Get Fit!*

Always Keep the Focus on the Positive

Again it is important to note that this is a cumulative school or team award. Administrators need to make sure that students know that this award is a group effort, with all of their teachers contributing to whether or not they get the award. Administrators need to also make sure that both staff and students know that we want to focus on the positives. Everyone should understand that a huge emphasis is going to be placed on improvement! For example, a student has been getting mostly thumbs down for his effort or behavior or both, and then just one of the teachers sees some improvement and is able to give the student thumbs up. The bulk of the teachers are still thumbs down, but looking at the whole student and the student's entire day, there has been some improvement in some part of the student's day. The administrator should encourage the teachers to always give this student the thumbs-up recognition.

To maximize the impact of this program, the leaders need to remind all of the teachers to make note of the thumbs up even though some of them were still not able to give the student a thumb up. In fact, the administrator needs to remind all of the thumbs-down teachers to make a concerted effort to mention the specific improvement the student has made in the one teacher's class. Therefore, as the student goes through the day after the Thumbs Meeting, every teacher is going to make a point of talking to the student about the improved efforts he or she has demonstrated for one of the other teachers. You can also bet that the administrator will also make a point of seeing the student sometime during the day and congratulating him or her on the improvement and award. Before the Thumbs-Up format, administrators had no organized way for teachers to share with each other the gradual improvement of every student, and to make sure that every student is being considered on a regular basis.

Sometimes the trick to motivating students is to know what a student is doing for the other teachers, and use that to motivate the student in your class. Using the Thumbs Meetings, administrators have a system where the teachers are interested in how students are doing in other classes and they are able to get input and share information about all of the students. Then they make decisions about positive reinforcement and interventions as a group. Notice that this system includes the Involvement Model of Change. Also notice that another one of the great things about this system is that it includes all of the students, and not just the ones causing the most trouble.

The administrative team now has a system that requires that each teacher always be looking for any way in which students have improved, and then be ready to share that improvement with other teachers. All of the teachers will then try to build on that improvement. Hopefully, with all of the teachers looking for any improvement, someone will see a positive behavior that is worth recognizing, and the rest of the teachers will also be able to build on this improvement.

Administrative teams will continually have to remind the staff that the process is dependent on teachers finding something constructive to input about a student. This means that the thumbs-up signal is not for making a particular grade, but for the effort a student is putting forth. Therefore, when teachers indicate a thumbs-down signal for a student, they are saying in effect that they have not seen anything redeeming from the student that would merit any recognition for the past two weeks. This puts the focus on finding improvement.

Many average and certainly most below average students have never received any formal recognition for their efforts, which is why they do not progress beyond a certain level. When they see that they can earn recognition for their efforts, and that the recognition is based on them continually trying to improve, it is not hard to imagine why these students begin to set higher goals. In fact that is true of all students; when schools systematically recognize their efforts to improve their work, they begin to set even higher goals. Setting goals is another big component of the Thumbs-Up system.

Setting Goals

Most schools like to have every student receive either a certificate of recognition or a notice of the need for improvement every two weeks. Regardless of whether there are actual certificates given out, most administrative teams ask the teachers to have the students fill out a goal sheet on a regular basis. This is often a part of advisory programs, and it is an integral part of the thumbs-up process. In most instances, the goal sheet is simply a half sheet of paper that says *MY GOAL FOR THE NEXT TWO WEEKS IS:* on which the students write their goal(s) for the next two weeks.

MY GOAL FOR THE NEXT TWO WEEKS IS:
_____
_____
_____
_____
_____
Student Name

Schools have found that they can keep students focused on a two-week goal more successfully than on monthly or longer goals. In this instance, the goal should be in reference to what the student needs to do to receive thumbs-up recognition at the next Thumbs Meeting. Leaders will need to work with the staff regarding helping students write goals. Teachers should remember that the goals should be achievable. The teachers should help the students set incremental goals for continuing to improve. Bringing up a low grade even a little bit *(maybe, especially a little bit!)* would be a great goal. Maintaining a good grade would also be a very good goal.

The administrative team will want to remind the staff and students that goals can also be getting involved with a service learning project, or service to the school such as helping other students by becoming a peer mentor. Of course, improving behavior would also be an appropriate goal for some students. We need to help students understand how the big goals are achieved by going through a lot of small goals along the way. The goal sheet can be as simple as a half-sheet of paper as shown on page 84.

The Encore (Elective or Exploratory) Teachers

The administrative team will have to facilitate the participation of the encore teachers in this process. The encore teachers often see a side of students that the core teachers do not. To get the complete picture of the whole student, the administrators need input from every teacher that works with the students. Administrators should set up a calendar so that encore teachers know when the various teams are going to run their Thumbs Meetings. The encore teachers can vote by proxy by sending the administrator, counselor, or team a list of the students they would give a thumbs down. Leaders should ask the encore teachers to go through their class list one student at a time just like the core team is going to do at the meeting, and consider the five criteria as they look at each name.

In most schools, the participation of encore teachers has become much easier because the lists can be sent electronically. Administrators should ask the encore teachers to simply put one or more of the words that describe problems by the students' names for which they have concerns. Then an administrator or counselor will follow-up with the encore teachers to get the specifics about the concerns. For example, the industrial technology teacher might indicate a student's name, and put the words "discipline" and "social" by the name. An administrator or counselor will stop by the teacher's room to get the specific disciplinary and social concerns and follow up accordingly.

Administrators know that some students perform better in the encore classes than in the core classes. So it can happen that a core team is having a difficult time finding that positive indicator for a student. If the encore teachers have not indicated a thumbs down for the student, the administrator, counselor, or one of the team members will contact the appropriate exploratory teachers to find some positive indicators that the core teachers can use. There are many occasions where the students earn an award because of what the students are doing in the encore classes. Then the core teachers can use the goal-setting process to get the students to begin to improve in those classes.

The Interventions

The group will have to hear why the thumbs-down signals were given to each student in order to determine appropriate interventions. The administrator will lead the group in reviewing the reasons given for the thumbs downs. The signals should be for one or more of the five criteria stated earlier: academic effort, behavior, and social, emotional, and personal issues. The administrator should ensure that this is a "group" decision regarding the best course of action for that student. The interventions will be based on the areas of concern expressed for each student.

Academic Effort

If a student's academic effort is one of the issues, there are several options for the team to consider. If the school has an advisory program, then the student's advisor will discuss with the student any academic concerns that have been expressed. This will be done with the student during the time when the teacher passes out the Thumbs-Up certificates and the Heads-Up notices. The teacher explains where the student needs to improve his or her academic efforts, and what the teachers decided would indicate at least some improvement for the student over the next two weeks. The teacher will help the student set appropriate, specific goals to determine improvement based on their discussion.

The counselor or teachers may also recommend additional tutoring in the after-school program. In that case, the advisor will contact the parents to see if the student can stay for the after-school program a few days a week. The team may also recommend a "Homework Pal" who checks with the student daily to make sure the student is prepared when he leaves school, and to double-check with the student in the mornings to get work completed as needed.

The administrator might suggest other interventions which might include additional help time during the lunch help time and getting the parents to sign the agenda book each day, indicating they have seen his assignments. The counselor might also get involved with the student and work on organizational skills. The idea is to get the interventions started at the first sign that the student is not performing academically as he or she should. It is also important to note that very often students will receive a thumbs-up award for improvement and still have several interventions as well.

Behavior— Proactive Student Management

If a student receives a thumbs-down signal for behavior, the administrator will usually take the lead. The administrator will ask the teachers to quickly list the behaviors that are causing the problems. The administrator will make notes about the behaviors and determine the best time for tracking down the student. Administrators need to know that the best places for proactive behavior discussions are the hallways as students are changing classes, in the cafeteria, in the morning as the students mingle before school, and at the end of one of the periods. *(What I would do is go into the class and sit by the student or call the student into the hallway. I always liked to talk to the students in the most public places possible. Remember administrators, this is not a referral and so the discussion can and should be brief.)* Discuss disciplinary concerns with the student and make suggestions for improving his or her behavior. The idea is to make contact and discuss the issues with students before they get to the referral stage of the discipline process.

I would tell the students what behaviors I had been made aware of, and in which classes I was concerned about their behavior. I would share what I wanted them to do to correct the situation, and then I would remind them that, just like the famous Arnold quote, "I'll be back!" This is very true, because in two weeks the teachers are going to read the class lists and go through the names again. The student will then earn a Thumbs-Up certificate or not. Either way, "I'll be back!"

The reason that I like to have very public places in which to talk to students about their behavior is that I also want it to be very public when I come back and shake the hands of the students that have improved their behavior. My personal experience has been that my follow-up meetings after my initial contacts are almost always very positive. Another bonus for administrators is the effect this system will have when you are doing your "rounds." As an administrator, I always visited every classroom every day, and I asked the other administrators to do the same. We would just step into each class and get a feeling for what was going on. I will tell you that after you have made your initial contacts following Thumbs Meetings and you look into classrooms, every one of those students you talked to will think you are coming into class just to check on them.

It is also critical that the counselor be involved with any students experiencing behavior difficulties. There are students making some bad choices and they may not realize the alternatives available. There may be some home issues that no one is aware of. It is just the nature of the school-age child that there are almost always social, emotional, or personal issues involved with misbehavior, and in those situations the counselor would be the best person to work with the student. As with the administrators, the earlier the counselor is involved with the student, the more positive the effect can be.

It is not rocket science that when schools begin to put the real focus on the positive reinforcements and early interventions, they tend to bring down the referral rate significantly. *(In my personal experience working with schools, it is not unusual at all for the written referral rate to drop by half. Of course, this is one of the reasons that grades will also go up significantly. The time teachers previously spent on discipline can now be put into instruction.)*

Social, Emotional, and Personal Issues

Administrators know that counselors can have a huge impact on students if they know which students need their help. Making social, emotional, and personal issues a part of the criteria gets the teachers thinking about those aspects of their students more regularly. The counselor should always be involved with any student experiencing behavior difficulties. The teachers should indicate a thumbs down if they have any feeling that something is not quite right with a student.

I tell teachers that "if the hairs on the back of your neck stand up when this student's name is mentioned," indicate thumbs down and let's talk about it. Of course, if the teachers think there is anything serious at all, they should contact a counselor or administrator right away.

I have been in many of these meetings where the teachers cannot articulate the specific issue. Teachers will say things like, "I am not sure, but Susie has not been participating like she usually does. Has anyone else noticed this?" This statement actually came during one of the Thumbs Meetings I attended as an administrator. Susie was usually the first student to raise her hand and she always volunteered to do work, and so on. She was one of the really great students we all wish we had all the time. The teacher had noticed that Susie was still doing well, but not nearly as enthusiastically as usual. Of course, this could indicate many different things during this time of a student's life. The teacher had asked Susie if anything was wrong, and she had said, "No."

So the situation was not one of immediate concern that would cause a teacher to go straight to the counselor's office to check on Susie. However, since every name is read out loud, this teacher indicated a thumbs down for Susie to see if anyone else had noticed this with Susie. If Susie's name had not been read aloud, this teacher may not have thought to bring up her name since she was a great student, and it was a subtle thing she was bringing up.

The response was another phrase often heard in these meetings, "Now that you mention it . . ." as another teacher realized that she had noticed what the previous teacher mentioned. In Susie's case, it was the Science Teacher that said, "Now that you mention it, Susie did not volunteer to lead a lab group this time, and she usually wants to lead her lab group. I didn't think anything about it at the time, but she has not been as into the lab as usual this week." The counselor said she would look into it. After that meeting, the counselor stepped into a couple of Susie's classes and noticed that she seemed distracted.

The next day the counselor talked with Susie as only this counselor could. After talking for a short while, Susie broke down crying and went with the counselor telling her that her dad had left, and her mom had said he was not coming back. Susie's mom told her that they were separated and they were not going to get back together. No one else knew about the situation at this juncture, and Susie did not know how to handle it. She was embarrassed, confused, and mad, and you can imagine *how all of her emotions were overwhelming her. Susie felt that she had the weight of the world on her shoulders. The counselor worked with Susie and her mom and was willing and able to provide a tremendous amount of support. The key had been finding out that Susie actually needed support. This is when the Thumbs Meetings make the effort more than worthwhile.*

In Conclusion

Hopefully, now you can see why I said this process might well be the definition of differentiated leadership. This is the most proactive student management system, as well as the most comprehensive, positive reinforcement system that I have encountered. Every student is considered, and teachers get input from all of the other teachers. The information shared allows the administrators, counselors, and teachers to make the most informed decisions about possible interventions. Everyone is focused on looking for positive indicators and gets a renewed look at the students every two weeks. It will become evident if a teacher has student management issues. Learning communities are about putting together systems that enable everyone in the community to learn from everyone else in the community, and this is differentiated leadership.

TAG . . . You're It!

Positive Student Management

Exercise One

The administrative team (remember this includes the counselors) should divide up the teams in the building and each meet with teams to introduce the Thumbs-up process. See if one or maybe even all of your teams will schedule a time with an administrator and the counselor to run through a Thumbs Meeting. Be patient and know that it will take some time at first; but as you practice and stick to the rules (like not talking during the first phase of the meeting), the meetings will run smoothly.

Exercise Two

Now that you have run a Thumbs Meeting, it is time to practice the follow-up with the students. Talk to each of the students with discipline issues, have teachers remind students of their academic progress, and ask the counselor to be involved. The teachers might also want to design some sort of certificates that will be given out to the students, especially if everyone intends to have more Thumbs Meetings. The administrators and counselors should meet with their teams to follow up and assess how the process worked.

Documenting Interventions and Student Management Strategies

☐ Teacher ☐ Team ☐ School

Student Behaviors

Possible Strategies Available

-
-
-
-
-
-
-

-
-
-
-
-
-
-

Strategy Attempted   Date   Result

_____
_____
_____
_____
_____
_____
_____
_____
_____
_____
_____
_____
_____
_____

CLASSROOM INTERVENTION RECORD

STUDENT:

DATE:

INAPPROPRIATE BEHAVIOR:

ACTIONS LEADING UP TO THE BEHAVIOR:

DATE	INTERVENTION ATTEMPTED	RESULT

ADDITIONAL INTERVENTIONS AVAILABLE

TEAM INTERVENTION RECORD

INAPPROPRIATE BEHAVIOR:

ACTIONS LEADING UP TO THE BEHAVIOR:

STUDENT:

DATE:

DATE	INTERVENTION ATTEMPTED	RESULT

ADDITIONAL INTERVENTIONS AVAILABLE

Positive Reinforcements and Rewards Record

Student Behavior

Reinforcements, Accommodations, and Rewards Available

Date	Rewards Offered	Result

_____
_____
_____
_____
_____
_____
_____
_____
_____
_____
_____
_____

Differentiated Leadership
Copyright ©2008 by Incentive Publications, Inc., Nashville, TN.

Flexible Schedules to Promote Differentiated Systems

Flexing Your Schedule

A big part of differentiated leadership is building a schedule that will allow and enable staff collaboration and development of programs that promote differentiated instruction and assessment. We know that whatever we do with the school schedule impacts all of the other systems. Changes in schedule are usually the most evident. Nothing determines how instruction and assessment are structured more than the master schedule. A schedule that is too tight restricts programs that promote differentiated instruction and assessment like teaming, authentic assessments, and integrated curriculums. So schools must schedule for maximum flexibility, and that will require a flexible block schedule with academies or teams.

> Nothing determines how instruction and assessment are structured more than the master schedule.

As the name implies, a flexible block schedule creates large "blocks" of instructional time that can be "flexed" by the teachers. A flexible block schedule allows and enables teachers to create differentiated instructional and assessment options. It is the most difficult schedule to build.

Putting together a differentiated group of teachers to utilize the instructional blocks requires structures like interdisciplinary academies or teams. An interdisciplinary academy or team is a common group of teachers from different content areas, who share a common group of students for an extended portion of the day. So the first step in developing a flexible block schedule is structuring and assembling interdisciplinary academies or teams.

Scheduling Academies or Teams

The mechanics of interdisciplinary teams requires extensive collaboration. For this collaboration to be successful, administrative teams need to be especially careful with the construction of academies and teams. So now we need to talk more about the people that will be making up these core academies and teams. I want to put teachers together on an academy or team that will complement each other's talents. Let's begin with the assignment of teachers to academies or teams, and then discuss how to build a schedule.

I will finish our discussion with the advantages and disadvantages of various team sizes, and another example of how the team can flex their instructional time. The word *academy* tends to be a high-school term, while middle schools tend to use the word *team*. For the purposes of this chapter, the terms are interchangeable. So for the rest of this chapter, I will use the word *team* in its various forms, which will, of course, also represent academy in kind.

When a school decides to go into teaming, one of the first causes of serious anxiety are the questions: What team I might get assigned to? Who will be my teammates? Those are important questions, as teams meet together often and have to deal with stressful situations. Teammates will have to support each other and learn to anticipate each other's moves, so it is critical that care be taken when assigning teachers to teams. Putting the right personalities together is important.

Selecting Teams

The process of selecting teams can be done in one of two ways. The first is let the teachers select the teams, and the second is to have team selection be an administrative task. In either instance, some sort of teacher survey must be used. The purpose of a survey is to solicit any teacher preferences, and any other information the selection committee or the administrative team deems necessary. This information might include teaching assignment preferences, certifications, teammate preferences, personality profiles, and teaching- and learning-style inventories.

Regardless of how the teams are selected, it is imperative that the teams are equal in every way possible. This would include an equal number of "weak" and "strong" teachers, a gender and racial balance reflective of the overall teaching staff, as well as a mix of teaching styles and personalities.

The question to ask the staff is, "If you had a child coming into the middle school at any of the grade levels, would you honestly be able to say that you would be just as happy (or sad) if your child was put on any of the teams?" After the teams are selected, ideally they should be perceived as equally strong.

Here are several possible ways to select teams:

★ 1   Use a Selection Committee

The selection committee should, of course, include representatives from each grade level, and administrators. The task of the committee will be to consider the surveys, look at the possible combination of teams, and come up with the most balanced teams possible. The good news is that you get input from colleagues who really know about each other. The bad news is that it puts teachers in a difficult position of saying what makes one team stronger or weaker than another. This can become a very political and personal situation for the teachers, and great care must be taken to keep feelings from getting hurt.

★ 2   Teachers Form Teams

An administrator once decided to totally empower the teachers. His teachers were requesting that they be actively involved, so he decided to have the teachers select the formation of the teams. What he did was to decide which eight teachers would be the sixth-grade teachers, which eight teachers would be the seventh-grade teachers, which eight teachers would be the eighth-grade teachers, and which teachers would be the exploratory teachers. He put the sixth-grade teachers in one room, the seventh-grade teachers in another room, and so on.

As he put each group in a classroom, he told them they were to form two four-person teams at each grade level, and that they could not come out until the task was done. While the grade level teachers were deciding on teams, he met with the exploratory teachers to go over the exploratory schedule and to explain how the exploratory teachers would be working as a team. The teachers had been told about balanced teams, and they did come up with a good combinations of teachers for the teams.

The problem with this method of having the teachers pick the teams is the potential for the playground syndrome, where someone is picked first, and someone is picked last. We all know which one we would hope to be, but it does not always work that way. In the example above, there were some hurt feelings among the teachers as they worked their way through the process of deciding who would teach with whom. The idea is to have ownership without creating a great deal of anxiety.

★ **3**   **Administrators Form Teams**

The other method of selecting teams is to make it an administrative function. The administrative team can select and assign the teams. This should also be with the input from the staff via some sort of survey. The empowerment is there through the surveys, but this method takes the teachers out of the selection process, and makes the process much less political within the staff. *(I suggest that there be staff discussion about all of the alternatives, and the team selection process should be a site-based decision.)*

And the Survey Says . . .

There are several surveys available for assisting in the team selection process. Find an existing survey. *(One good example is in the resource book* The Definitive Middle School Guide.*)* Use this or another survey, or you can customize one to meet your particular needs. There is a variety of information you may want to include in your survey. Let the staff know that the surveys will be kept in the strictest of confidence and include the categories of information that will help choose successful groupings.

- preferences for subject-area teaching assignments

- discipline philosophies

- results of personality profiles like "True Colors" and "Myers-Briggs"

- results of teaching- and learning-style inventories like "FourMat"

The idea is not to put all teachers of like personalities or teaching styles together, but rather to get a diverse group of teachers together. The more diverse the teachers are that make up a team, the greater the potential strength of the team. This provides for a wider variety of views.

Size Matters

The next question is team size. *(And one size definitely does not fit all.)* Team size depends on many factors, including how many sections of each class are at a grade level, what the certifications of the teachers are, and philosophical considerations of small or large teams. The number of sections at a grade level determines the magic number for team size, as the size of each team has to add up to that number. For example, if you have eight sections in a grade level, you could have several different configurations of team sizes. You might have two four-person teams, or you might have two three-person teams and one two-person team, or you could also have four two-person teams. Any combination is possible as long as the total number of teachers on all of teams adds up to eight. Different team sizes with more examples are discussed later in this chapter.

The certifications of the teachers determine how they can be placed on a team, and affect the possibilities for team size. For example, if a teacher is secondary certified in math only, that teacher has to be on a team at the seventh or eighth grade level and can teach only one subject, which is math; so this teacher needs to be on a large team to fill a day with math classes.

As you will see, smaller teams require teachers to teach more than one subject. A teacher with multiple certifications or an elementary certification could be on a smaller team. Some schools prefer smaller teams because the teachers can get to know the students better, while others feel larger teams help with the transition to high school and college. As you consider various team size options, it is important to understand that there are advantages and disadvantages for any team size.

There will always be good news and bad news in every situation. This seems to be especially true in the field of education and more so still with the scheduling process. Sometimes the good news is also the bad news. For example: the good news is there are a lot of possible combinations for putting teams together; the bad news is there are a lot of possible combinations for putting teams together.

Consider the large number of combinations that are possible if we have 12 sections at a grade level. For example, six two-person teams or four three-person teams or two six-person teams. To make things more interesting, you could also have combinations of two five-person teams and one two-person team, and so on. Again, unless we have cross-grade-level teams, team sizes must add up to the number of sections offered for each core subject at each grade level.

So, to help you decide which combinations might work best, here's the good news and the bad news about each team size.

(Generally I do not recommend very large teams, but they may be unavoidable due to certification issues. I have found that with training and teacher commitment, even larger teams can be very successful.)

TWO-PERSON TEAMS

THE GOOD NEWS

- More time with each student due to smaller group of students (Two sections means teams are usually between 50 and 60 students.)
- Consensus is easier to reach with two teachers.
- Students will benefit from better relationships with teachers. Since they have each teacher more than once each day, they get to know their teachers much better.
- Teachers get to know parents much better.
- Fewest discipline problems
- Easiest model for integrating the curriculum
- Field trips are easier to organize.
- Easiest team size for scheduling common preparation time and creating true teams
- Easiest model to "FLEX" instructional time

THE BAD NEWS

- Only two teachers to share the workload and generate ideas. (It's either you or me.)
- With only two sections of students, there are fewer opportunities for regrouping students.
- Each teacher has to prepare to teach more than one class. (Teachers will have at least two, usually three, and occasionally four preparations.)
- If there are leveled classes, this may create some tracking.
- No one to play the mediator for the teachers

THREE-PERSON TEAMS

THE GOOD NEWS

- More time with each student with a moderate size group of students (There are usually between 75 and 90 students on the team.)
- Consensus is still relatively easy to reach with three teachers, and one can play mediator when needed.
- Students can benefit from three teaching styles.
- Easy to integrate the curriculum as there is at least one shared subject
- Teachers get to know parents well.
- Fewer discipline problems than with larger teams
- Still easy to schedule common preparation time
- Easy to "FLEX" instructional time
- Three teachers to share the work load

THE BAD NEWS

- Conflicts can produce a "two against one" feeling between the teachers.
- Teachers still have multiple preparations for classes. (Although teachers generally have only two preparations, they can occasionally have three.)
- More flexibility than two-person teams, but still only three potential classroom groupings for students
- Leveled classes may still cause tracking of students.

FOUR-PERSON TEAMS

THE GOOD NEWS

- Fewer teacher preparations allow for more specialization which usually allows for teachers to focus on the state standards for only one area. (Teachers often have only one preparation, occasionally two.)
- Four teachers to share the workload and generate ideas
- Easier to accommodate leveled classes, such as math, and avoid tracking
- More opportunities for grouping and regrouping students
- More negotiation required, but still relatively easy to "FLEX" instructional time

THE BAD NEWS

- Achieving consensus takes longer than with the smaller teams.
- More difficult to integrate the curriculum with each teacher most often specializing and working in only one area
- Less time with each student because there are more students to work with (usually between 100 and 120)
- More discipline than with smaller teams
- Difficult to organize whole team field trips and other activities

FIVE-PERSON TEAMS

THE GOOD NEWS

- Fewer teacher preparations will allow teachers to focus on the state standards for only one area. (Teachers usually have only one preparation and occasionally two.)
- Five teachers to share the workload and generate ideas
- Very easy to accommodate leveled classes and avoid tracking, with five opportunities for grouping and regrouping students
- Opportunity to add subject(s) to a team in addition to math, science, language arts, and social studies (like reading or an exploratory class)

THE BAD NEWS

- It is more difficult to get input from all teachers during a team meeting; therefore, achieving consensus requires much more work and team meetings can take longer.
- Much less time with each student because of the large number of students to work with (usually between 125 and 150 students)
- More difficult to integrate the curriculum as teachers work in one content area
- Requires five subjects to build the team (have to add a class like reading or an exploratory rotation class)
- Can be difficult to schedule a common preparation
- Much more difficult to get to know all students and parents well
- More discipline problems
- More difficult to organize whole-team field trips and other activities
- More difficult to "FLEX" instructional times, as there are more classes and students to consider

SIX-PERSON TEAMS

THE GOOD NEWS

- Fewer teacher preparations, almost always only one for which to be responsible

- Six teachers to share the work and generate ideas

- Easy to accommodate leveled classes and avoid tracking

- Six opportunities for grouping and regrouping students into classes

THE BAD NEWS

- More difficult to get input from all teachers during a team meeting; therefore, achieving consensus requires much more work, and team meetings take longer

- Substantially less time with each student because of very large number of students to work with (usually between 150 and 180 students)

- Much more difficult to integrate the curriculums as teachers work in one area, and there are many more teachers with whom to make a connection

- Requires six subjects to build the team (usually there will be another core class like reading and an exploratory teacher attached to the team on a rotating basis)

- Very difficult to block all the students with the team (Often one or more sections of students are "off-team" which makes flexing the instructional time impossible.)

- Very difficult to "FLEX" instructional time (In addition to trying to coordinate with more teachers, the schedule often will not accommodate flexing; see above.)

- Having substantially more students usually implies more discipline problems.

- More difficult to discuss all of the students, and make adequate parent contacts

Team Size—The Final Word

When putting teams together, philosophy and practical reality often butt heads with each other. You may want to have the smaller teams philosophically, but the practical matter of teacher certification or the number of sections available may get in the way. For example, let's look at what happens in a school where teachers teach six of eight periods each day and there are singularly certified staff members. A secondary certified math teacher will have to be on a seventh or eighth grade team because of the certification.

That means that this teacher certified only in secondary math must teach all of the periods in math. You will see in the examples below that this teacher must be on a five- or six-person team, in order to facilitate the teacher's assignment to math classes only. If he or she teaches on a smaller team, there simply are not enough sections of math to fill the day. This situation often results in math being off the team, or cross-teaming, which of course is not really teaming.

The examples below show how teams could be scheduled and the math teacher assigned. In figure T-1, you will see how the teacher fits in a five- or six-person team. In figure T-2, the teacher is shared between two three-person teams (a cross-teaming situation). *(At the end of the chapter, you will have a chance to try different combinations for your own school.)*

(Figure T-1)

Six-Person Team and Five-Person Team Examples in an Eight-Period Schedule with Two Planning Periods

6-PERSON TEAM								
	1	2	3	4	5	6	7	8
1. Debra	P	P	MA	MA	MA	MA	MA	MA
2. Pat	L	L	LA	LA	LA	LA	LA	LA
3. Donald	A N	A N	SS	SS	SS	SS	SS	SS
4. Gene	N	N	SCI	SCI	SCI	SCI	SCI	SCI
5. Freddy	I	I	RDG	RDG	RDG	RDG	RDG	RDG
6. Rodney	N G	N G	PE/ HLTH	PE/ HLTH	PE/ HLTH	PE/ HLTH	PE/ HLTH	PE/ HLTH

Notice that reading and PE/health teachers are the fifth and sixth members of the team. Any exploratory class like art might be attached as well. At semester's end the exploratory teacher could rotate to a different team. This is a great way to get the exploratory teachers greatly involved with the core teams.

5-PERSON TEAM								
	1	2	3	4	5	6	7	8
1. Debra	P L A N N I N G	P L A N N I N G	MA	MA	MA	MA	MA
2. Pat			LA	LA	LA	LA	LA
3. Donald			SS	SS	SS	SS	SS
4. Gene			SCI	SCI	SCI	SCI	SCI
5. Freddy			RDG	RDG	RDG	RDG	RDG

In this example, the core teachers teach only five sections in the same time frame in which they would have taught six. So if each of the periods were originally 45 minutes with five-minute passing, each core class would now be 56 minutes with five-minute passing. The good news is more time in each core class. The bad news is that since core teachers are teaching one less section each, a few more staff members will be required.

(Figure T-2)
Examples with Three-person Teams in an Eight-period Schedule with Two Planning Periods

3-PERSON TEAM (Example 1)								
	1	2	3	4	5	6	7	8
1. Debra	P L A N	P L A N	MA	MA	MA	SCI	SCI	SCI
2. Pat			LA	LA	LA	RDG	RDG	RDG
3. Donald			SS	SS	SS	PE/HLTH	PE/HLTH	PE/HLTH

Notice that each teacher on this three-person team has two different classes to prepare for. While there are many advantages to this team, each teacher must be certified to teach two subjects.

3-PERSON TEAM (Example 2)								
	1	2	3	4	5	6	7	8
1. Debra	P L A N	P L A N	MA	MA	MA	RDG	SCI
2. Pat			LA	LA	LA	RDG	SCI
3. Donald			SS	SS	SS	RDG	SCI

In this example, more time is spent in each of the core classes. Each teacher has three classes to prepare and certification is still an issue. The extra time may help with state assessment scores, but as before, it comes with a cost of more staff and more teacher prep time. *(Note: It is possible that two of the teachers could have two preparations with the third having three preparations.)*

Filling In the Blanks

Regardless of the team size, each line has to be filled in, and each teacher has to teach as many classes as directed by the school district. After deciding how many classes each teacher has to teach, and what the certifications issues are, it is a matter of filling in the blanks to form teams. It is important to note that all teams in a building do not have to be the same size.

Choreographing and Training for the Program

The Common Planning Period

The common planning period is absolutely critical if teams are to function at the highest possible level. The best circumstance for teams is to have both an individual planning period and a team planning period. In a two-planning-period model, teachers will have a period to meet with their team. It should be noted that because of planning with a team, teachers will also be able to make better use of their individual planning time.

During team time, teachers will be able address student issues more effectively and eliminate some of the duplicated efforts they all perform. When teachers plan for an integrated curriculum as a team, they will greatly improve their planning for individual classroom instruction as learning connections are developed.

Teachers have so much "administrivia" to take care of, it can leave little time to actually plan for instruction. Working as a team during a team planning period will allow teachers to spend more of their individual planning getting ready for their classes. For example, consider the contacting of parents. One team member can call parents after a team meeting and represent several classes. This saves the parents from getting several calls in one evening, and saves time for several of the teachers. In this way, teams can actually make considerably more parent contacts than if teachers worked in isolation, because they share the calling duties and parent information.

In their individual planning periods, teachers previously had to work independently to address all student issues. Now teachers can address most, if not all, student issues during team time, and get a consensus approach to solving student situations. This frees up the individual planning for actually preparing for instruction. In a teamed model, teachers will be planning for interdisciplinary instruction as well as individual instruction. This all means that in a teamed model, teachers will actually do more instructional planning than ever for their individual classes.

The common planning period is filled every day with topics that include student issues, interdisciplinary curriculum development, building the small community for learning, planning for advisory, planning for team events, meeting with administrators and counselors, and on and on. *(A complete list of team meeting topics and sample agendas can be found in the books* Get Fit! *and* WOW, What A Team!*)*

I fully understand the budget constraints of many school districts and realize providing two planning periods simply may not be fiscally feasible. Teaming can happen without a team planning period; however, the teams will be very limited in what they can realistically be expected to accomplish. The bottom line is that, whenever possible, teachers should have a common team planning period in addition to the individual planning period, and the importance of having both planning periods cannot be overstated.

Placing the Planning Periods

When it is possible to have both a common and a team planning period, it is also very important that the two planning periods be scheduled back to back. This has several benefits, and the first is to the exploratory team. The core team has planning when students are in the exploratory classes. Putting the team and individual planning periods back to back lets the exploratory teachers have the same students for two periods in a row. Now the exploratory teachers will have a series of two-period instructional blocks that they can also flex as a team.

For the core teachers, having the personal and team planning periods back to back means that they will have more versatile use of both the planning block and the instructional block. Splitting up the planning periods also means splitting up the instructional block. When you throw lunch into the schedule, you can split up the instructional day as many as four times, which will really limit the number of ways a team can flex their instructional time. Figure T-3 represents the schedule before I worked with the school to add flexibility to the schedule. Figure T-4 is the schedule we were able to create.

In the *Before* schedule, I want you to notice how chopped up the instructional blocks are for the teams, and how spread out the exploratory classes are. The only possible advantage is that teachers are off at different times throughout the day, but it makes flexing time nearly impossible. Therefore, this schedule is not a very good schedule for students at all.

In the *After* schedule, the team and individual planning periods are together. Notice that the smallest instructional block is two periods, and many are three or more. This will give everyone in the building the greatest opportunity to be creative with his or her instructional time. None of the following examples of flexing the schedule are possible in the *Before* schedule. However, if the administration thinks about specific team situations and practices differentiated leadership, all of the examples along with many more possibilities can be implemented in the *After* schedule.

Figure T-3   BEFORE

	5th Grade	6th Grade	7th Grade	8th Grade
1	Exploratory Class / Core Team Planning	CORE BLOCK	CORE BLOCK	CORE BLOCK
2	CORE BLOCK	CORE BLOCK	CORE BLOCK	Exploratory Class / Core Team Planning
3	CORE BLOCK	CORE BLOCK	Exploratory Class / Core Team Planning	CORE BLOCK
4	CORE BLOCK	Exploratory Class / Core Team Planning	CORE BLOCK	CORE BLOCK
5	Exploratory Class / Core Team Planning	BLOCK	LUNCH	CORE BLOCK
	LUNCH	LUNCH	CORE BLOCK	LUNCH
6	CORE BLOCK	CORE BLOCK	Exploratory Class / Core Team Planning	CORE BLOCK
7	CORE BLOCK	CORE BLOCK	CORE BLOCK	Exploratory Class / Core Team Planning
8	CORE BLOCK	Exploratory Class / Core Team Planning	CORE BLOCK	CORE BLOCK

Figure T-4   AFTER

	5th Grade	6th Grade	7th Grade	8th Grade
1	Exploratory Block / Core Team Planning	Core BLOCK	Core BLOCK	Core BLOCK
2	Exploratory Block / Core Team Planning	Core BLOCK	Core BLOCK	Core BLOCK
3	Core BLOCK	Core BLOCK	Exploratory Block / Core Team Planning	Core BLOCK
4	Core BLOCK	Core BLOCK	Exploratory Block / Core Team Planning	Core BLOCK
5	Core BLOCK	Exploratory Block / Core Team Planning	LUNCH	LUNCH
	LUNCH	LUNCH	Core BLOCK	Core BLOCK
6	Core BLOCK	Exploratory Block / Core Team Planning	Core BLOCK	Core BLOCK
7	Core BLOCK	Core BLOCK	Core BLOCK	Exploratory Block / Core Team Planning
8	Core BLOCK	Core BLOCK	Core BLOCK	Exploratory Block / Core Team Planning

Notice how the schedule in figure T-3 has many short, equal-length periods. In T-4 the individual and team planning periods are back-to-back. The long instructional blocks in T-4 give teachers more continuous instructional time, which is critical to flexibility. Now, the creativity of the teachers is the only limit to the scheduling possibilities. *(With our creative teachers, this means there is no limit to the possibilities!)*

The Exploratory Team

With the planning periods back-to-back, the exploratory team may decide to run double blocks on an "A-B" type of schedule for a few days for a special unit. This way they only have to get materials out once for each group or grade level, instead of many more times during the day (three times instead of six). We also suggest that each section of exploratory be scheduled by team. That way, the exploratory teachers are not always left with part of a class every time any team takes a field trip. By the way, since the exploratory team will be coordinating with all teams regarding students and curriculum, it also important that they have a team planning in addition to a personal planning period.

Now Let's Flex Some More!

Now that you know how to put the teams together, and the schedule looks great, let's look at three more ways to make the most of the flexibility. They demonstrate how the schedule can allow and enable differentiated instruction and assessment. Without a flexible block schedule, these examples are impossible. This is also why we need **differentiated** leadership!

In the first example, I want to demonstrate how the team can make time for activities that do not fit any one of the content areas, but that are valuable and important to instruction. The administrative team practicing differentiated leadership can lend a hand not only to help with instruction, but also to give the team additional planning time.

Show a demonstration video or have a guest speak once to the entire team

One team I have worked with has an outstanding interdisciplinary unit based on "Cemeteries." One of their activities is showing the movie "The Lion King" to demonstrate the cycle of life. The movie is quite appropriate and motivating for the instructional unit, but does not fit any one of the content areas. *(Note: this example could work for a guest speaker as*

Differentiated Leadership
Copyright ©2008 by Incentive Publications, Inc., Nashville, TN.

well.) So instead of showing the movie for multiple days in one content area, team members show the movie to the entire team in one afternoon. On that day, they run shortened periods in the morning so that they will still be able to see all of their students.

In this building the administrative team practices differentiated leadership and is always looking for ways to help teams. In fact, the administrative team will meet the students in the auditorium and the administrators will show the movie. While the administrative team monitors the students during the movie, they give the team of teachers a little more planning time. The team of teachers will meet to plan activities and assessments for the next unit or finalize the planning for the current unit. Talk about a win-win situation!

If it were the eighth-grade team shown in the example above, they might see all of their students during the morning block. To do this, they may have to run 35-minute periods, but they will see all of their students. Then the team will show the movie in the after lunch block. See the example in Figure T-5 below. In this case, the students will go from the movie to their exploratory classes. This means the teachers can have the entire afternoon for planning. This is a great example of how the administrative team can often help teams make the most of their time.

Figure T-5

Flexing the schedule to accommodate a video or speaker

	5th Grade	6th Grade	7th Grade	8th Grade
1	Exploratory Block / Core Team Planning	Core BLOCK	Core BLOCK	Periods 1–6 will happen in the morning block. Each period will be 35 minutes to allow the teachers to see all of the students. The movie will be shown in the afternoon block.
2				
3	Core BLOCK			
4			Exploratory Block / Core Team Planning	
5		Exploratory Block / Core Team Planning		
	LUNCH	LUNCH	LUNCH	LUNCH
6	Core BLOCK	Exploratory Block / Core Team Planning	Core BLOCK	Team will show the movie during this part of the Core Block.**
7		Core BLOCK		Exploratory Block / Core Team Planning
8				

** *If the administrative team shows the movie, this becomes additional planning time for the team!*

Flexing for Authentic Assessment Options

There are many teams that already give most of their tests as common team tests. For example, this might mean that the entire team will give the upcoming social studies test at the same time so that all students are taking the test the first thing in the block. Not only is this more brain appropriate, it also helps the students become more comfortable with the state testing format. Imagine using the flexible schedule to give an authentic assessment.

Setting up the Authentic Assessment

The science teacher is beginning the unit on biomes and she tells the students that they are going to have five ways to demonstrate their knowledge at the end of the unit. The students may choose between making a collage, doing a drawing or painting, building a physical model, telling about the biomes using a tape recorder, or writing a song about the biomes. She demonstrates and goes over the grading rubric for each. She lets them know that they have to be creating their product as they go through the lessons.

For the collage, the students need to be collecting their pictures and going over them with the teacher as they progress through the lessons. On test day, the students should only be putting the finishing touches onto their collages. The same goes for the drawings and paintings. The students should be checking their drawings as they go through the lessons, so that on the test day they are only adding the final thoughts.

The students that will be telling the teacher about the biomes via a tape recorder will be creating their script as they go through the lessons. On test day, they are only reading their finalized script which the teacher has already approved. The very same thing applies to writing a song. The students should have picked their song and have been adding their lyrics as they were going through the lessons. On test day, they are just recording their masterpiece. This way the students are even more attentive as the teacher goes through the lessons so that they can decide what part of the information needs to be included in their final project.

As the test day nears, the science teacher informs her teammates about the assessments. She will have the students split into five groups, and each of the teachers on the team will have one of the groups in his or her room. One teacher will have the students with the pictures, glue, and poster boards to complete their collages. Another teacher will have the students finishing up their drawings or paintings in her room. The science teacher will have the students building a physical model, and the students with their scripts or songs will go to other rooms.

Having all of the different assessments going on in one room would be very difficult at best, but sharing the process of administering the assessments makes it actually quite simple. Authentic assessments are powerful tools to use, but they are very labor-intensive for the teacher trying to implement them. You not only have to create the assessment formats, you will also have to create rubrics and grade five very different kinds of projects. *(I suggest that each teacher on the team try to develop one authentic assessment per semester. That way, students get the advantages of authentic assessments several times a semester, but each teacher only has to do it once. Once again, teaming pays huge benefits!)*

Making the Authentic Assessment Work

Suppose each teacher on the team teaches five of the seven daily periods as shown below, and each of the periods is 55 minutes long, with five minutes of passing time between each period. This gives the teachers 300 minutes of flexible time, including the class and passing times.

The first row shows a regular day with students going to exploratory classes during periods six and seven. Teachers take 30 minutes for the assessment first thing in the block for several days. That will leave them with 270 minutes for five periods and passing times ($270 \div 5 = 54$). Therefore, classes will be 54 minutes minus the passing. If five minutes is designated for passing, the classes will be 49 minutes each.

The second row reflects the different schedule for students on that day. Notice that whatever the team does with their time in the core block, the time to go to exploratory classes does not change. Also, we did not put in lunch, which could go anywhere within the core block.

Fig T-6 The top schedule is the regular schedule for the team, while the second row reflects what the schedule will look like on the day of the team authentic assessment.

Core Classes 55 minutes with five-minute passing		Exploratory Classes
Common Assessment 60 minutes	Core Classes 48 minutes	Exploratory Classes

Extended Learning Time

How can a team create **extended learning time** for their classes? The easiest example of this is a schedule where teachers teach six periods in an eight-period school day. Teachers see half of their classes on one day (the A day) and the other half of their students on the next day (the B day). In a traditional eight-period schedule, with 45-minute classes and three-minute passing periods, the core teachers would have six 45-minute periods each day. In an A–B schedule, the teachers would teach three 95-minute classes each day.

Regular Schedule		A–B Schedule	
Periods are 45 minutes long.		*Periods are 95 minutes long.*	
Monday	1-2-3-4-5-6	A day	1-2-3
Tuesday	1-2-3-4-5-6	B day	4-5-6
Wednesday	1-2-3-4-5-6	A day	1-2-3
Thursday	1-2-3-4-5-6	B day	4-5-6
Friday	1-2-3-4-5-6	A day	1-2-3
Monday	1-2-3-4-5-6	B day	4-5-6

Note that teachers see students three times one week, then two times the following week. Half of the passing times are eliminated and all of that time goes into instruction. Hallway issues are also cut in half. Teachers grade half as many papers each day, and students have half as much work to do each day.

Creating an A–B schedule is easy when teachers teach an even number of periods, but I promised you extreme flexibility! What if teachers teach five periods instead of six? In this instance teachers have 48-minute periods with a three-minute passing time. That means the core block is a total of 255 minutes long. Simply divide the core block into three periods instead of five. Dividing the time by three instead of five increases the instructional time for each block. Each teacher sees each class for three 81-minute periods per week.

When teachers see three groups of students a day instead of five, they eliminate two passing times, and the time gained goes directly into instructional time. This is often called a **modified block** and translates into extra instructional time. Teachers have less "administrivia" like taking roll and passing out materials. The schedule below shows a schedule for extended learning time for teachers teaching five periods a day, very popular for teachers wanting more instructional time.

Modified Block

Benefits include:

	DAY	PERIOD
• Increased instructional time		
• Some passing time goes into instruction	Mon	1-2-3
• Teachers can use more instructional strategies	Tue	4-5-1
• Students spend less time in the hallways	Wed	2-3-4
• Fewer papers for teachers to grade daily	Thu	5-1-2
• Fewer assignments for students per day	Fri	3-4-5

The teachers rotate their periods seeing each class three times each week. The three periods a day are 81 minutes each with a three-minute passing period.

TAG . . . You're It!

Flexing Your Schedule

Exercise One:

If your school has interdisciplinary teams, the administrative team should look at the current master schedule and determine if the team planning periods are positioned to create the largest instructional blocks possible. What changes might add flexibility to the schedule?

Exercise Two:

If your school does not have teams, the administrative team should determine how the current schedule might be divided into instructional blocks. Consideration should be given to how the exploratory classes would be scheduled to create the core blocks.

Exercise Three:

In this chapter, you read several examples of developing extended learning time. The idea is to see the students in larger instructional blocks. The teachers see each student fewer times each week, but for longer periods of time in each class. This type of schedule will net teachers and students additional instructional and assessment time. This also allows the teachers to utilize a much greater variety of instructional and assessment options. Work as an administrative team to build a model of extended learning time options for your school. This might be an A–B schedule, a rotation, or some other option.

Exercise Four:

If your school is going to be putting teachers into teams for the first time, or if there will be changes in team assignments due to changes in enrollment, you will enjoy this exercise. Below are blank templates for two-person through six-person teams. You can write in sample names to see how you might distribute the core classes that have to be taught in your school depending on the team size. You can use real or make-believe names; however, you will want to use the certifications issues in your building to see how certifications work out with different combinations of teachers.

The charts specify an eight-period day; however, you can also easily adapt them to a six- or seven-period day by marking out the last one or two columns as needed. Simply duplicate each form as many times as necessary for the number of teams you will need.

Two-person Team

Name	1	2	3	4	5	6	7	8
1.								
2.								

Three-person Team

Name	1	2	3	4	5	6	7	8
1.								
2.								
3.								

Four-person Team

Name	1	2	3	4	5	6	7	8
1.								
2.								
3.								
4.								

Five-person Team

Name	1	2	3	4	5	6	7	8
1.								
2.								
3.								
4.								
5.								

Six-person Team

Name	1	2	3	4	5	6	7	8
1.								
2.								
3.								
4.								
5.								
6.								

Motivating Your Staff with Differentiated Leadership

Finding the Right Motivators

Differentiated leadership requires that administrative teams do whatever it takes to motivate and engage every member of the staff. This is not an easy task. There are staff members in every school ready to go to mat for the leadership. There are also staff members at every school that are ready, and most often willing, to pull the mat out from under the leadership. Everything in this book is about finding ways to get all of the staff members invested in the school's success. The idea is to help everyone in the building learn and grow.

> Motivate and engage every member of your staff.

Over the years, I have had teachers that were thought to be simply negative. Some call them blockers, others antagonists, and Neila Connors simply calls them "Quackers"! Regardless of the name that is assigned to these staff members, the question is "How do you deal with them?" I have found that good people in bad systems sometimes come off as negative, and the system is just as much at fault. I am happy to report that, more often than not, the right actions by the administrative team can bring out the spark in many of the most negative staff. In this book, I am going to share systems and strategies to help administrative teams practice differentiated leadership.

Putting Brain Research to Work

Consider what educators know about brain research and the multiple intelligences. As administrators we certainly want our teachers to design lessons using multiple strategies so that they will appeal to various types of learners. For teachers, it is about finding the right motivators for the students. One motivator will work with one student, while another student needs a completely different motivator.

While teachers search for the right motivators, they might view some students more negatively. Once they find the right motivators and get the student performing, it is amazing how their attitude toward that student changes. *(More importantly to me is how the student's attitude will change in regards to the teacher, and in fact to the school as a whole.)* As administrators, we try to assist the teachers to continue to work with students until they find success.

Finding the right motivators is just as important for the staff as it is for the students. Some teachers perceived as the most negative have shown themselves to be anything but negative when properly engaged in systems that motivate and provide them the appropriate support. This book is about support systems that help teachers flourish.

I like to tell teachers that some students succeed "because of what you do," and some students succeed "in spite of what you do." As a teacher, I always strived to make it as much of the first case as possible.

The administrative teams need to know that this is also the same situation for teachers in your building. Some teachers flourish and succeed "because of what you do" while some teachers succeed "in spite of what you do" (and I would add "don't do"). As an administrator, I also wanted it be the first case for as much of the staff as possible. It is with that end in mind that I will begin with staff activities that are correlated to the multiple intelligences.

When I work with teachers in differentiated instruction workshops, I tell them that it is important to get the students "invested" in the class and their learning. For administrators, it is important for everyone involved in your school to be "invested" in your program. When people are involved in activities in the school, their level of investment goes up. Sometimes, it is simply a matter of finding the right activities for the staff to be involved in. Not everyone is up for working in the food concession at athletic events. As schools add various types of activities for the staff involvement, they often are pleasantly surprised to find interest in places they least expected it.

Something for Everyone via the Multiple Intelligences!

Many activities will appeal to more than one of the multiple intelligences, and of course, a person will have preferences in more than one of the intelligences. That is why the administrative team should work to provide as many options for staff participation as possible, like the ones I will share here.

Note to Administrators: the Curriculum & Project Planner for Integrating Multiple Intelligences, Thinking Skills (featuring Bloom's & Williams' Taxonomies), and Authentic Instruction *by Sandra Schurr (Incentive Publications) is a comprehensive list of assessments, actions, and learning tasks for each of the nine multiple intelligences. While the lists are comprehensive, the publication itself is only an eight-page fold-out. It is quite handy when planning for staff and parent meetings.*

Word Smart

Verbal–Linguistic

Verbs That Describe Verbal–Linguistic Behaviors:

adapt, argue, convince, create, critique, debate, describe, discuss, explain, interpret, interview, present, rewrite, synthesize, and teach

General Staff Responsibilities Appropriate for Staff Members with a Verbal–Linguistic Preference

☐ Help publish a school and/or team and/or departmental newsletter

☐ Create a "Featured Teacher" section in the local newspaper to highlight a teacher each week

☐ Send articles to the local newspaper to highlight student and teacher achievements

☐ Help design school and/or team and/or grade level and/or department letterheads

☐ Be a team leader and/or department head and/or committee chairperson

☐ Discuss and develop interdisciplinary learning connections as indicated on curriculum maps

☐ Be a part of the interview committee

☐ Help bring in motivational speakers for the students and staff

☐ Help put together school board presentations to highlight school achievements

☐ Help put together parent presentations for Parent Nights to highlight school and student achievements

☐ Help put together the team and/or departmental and/or administrative team résumés

☐ Help create team or school postcards to send to parents highlighting student achievements

☐ Work on developing a staff and student reward/recognition system

☐ Work on the student or teacher handbook committee

Specific Projects Begging for Staff Members with Verbal–Linguistic Talents

Help put together the team, departmental, or administrative team résumés

This is a fun activity and it is a great way to help your staff find out a little about each other. I use the résumés to introduce the administrative team, departments, teams, committees, and so on, at such functions as school board meetings and parent nights. It never fails that the résumés really impress whatever groups I share them with in talking about the school. I also find that some staff members really get into putting the résumés together.

Here is how the group résumés work. First the group decides what information to include on their résumé. They are going to 'pool" the information to create one cumulative résumé that will represent them as a group. Since educators have to have pretty good résumés to be in education, you can imagine how impressive it is to create a cumulative résumé. At school board meetings or parent nights or for the newspaper, I will say or write something like *"This is the math department. In the math department we have . . . "* and list the names, *"and they have . . . "* and I will start the résumé, which might begin with something like *" . . . 16 degrees from six different colleges, and they . . . "* and so on.

Of course, they will want the typical professional information like college degrees, certifications, professional organizations they are members of, any extracurricular activities they have been or currently are involved with, how many years total they have in education and/or how many students they have taught, and so on. *(These pooled group numbers can be incredibly large! This way I can say that a group has 45 years of teaching experience and not have to confess that it is really two rookies and a burn-out! Of course you know that I am just kidding.)*

Then the group should include some of their personal interests like hobbies, and so forth. Here they might include sports, gardening, reading, and so on. They should also include some of the jobs they have had outside of education. Some groups will include things like number of pets *(husbands are not to be included)*. You get the idea.

With the group résumés, people can share things and not worry about being singled out, as it is never revealed which person had which job, and so forth. My groups get to know a little about each other in a very nonthreatening way, I am given a great method of introducing my staff (including the administrative team), and the group résumés are fun in addition to being very impressive.

> **Help put together school board (and parent) presentations to highlight school achievements**

I recommend to administrative teams that they present regularly at school board meetings. In fact, I would have something to present to every school board meeting. There will always be numerous things that your school could be bragging about; it is just making it happen. If the administrative team will simply put together a calendar of the school board meetings at the beginning of the school year, they can create a "sign-up" sheet to go along with the calendar.

The administrative team should have teachers sign up for various times of the school year when they will provide something that could be shared at a school board meeting. The administrative team will make the presentations if needed (they often have to be there anyway), but the staff has to provide something for the leaders to highlight from their classes. For example: PowerPoint slides of student activities work really well. Initially it can be by department, and then by team or even individual teachers. What I find is that once departments, teams, or even individual teachers start providing things for the administrative team to present, the other teachers do not want to be outdone! Also, you find that most often the staff that is doing the sharing wants to help with the presentation at the school board meeting. It is, after all, they and their students that are being highlighted!

The administrative team should rotate the personal responsibility *(There will be more on personal responsibilities later.)* of making sure that the presentation for the next school board meeting is being prepared. There is a differentiated staff and parent meeting form on page ____ that will assist in the preparation of the presentation.

Number Smart

Logical– Mathematical

Verbs That Describe Logical–Mathematical Behaviors:
analyze, brainstorm, compare, compute, deduce, demonstrate differentiated, recognize patterns, integrate, observe, outline, and simplify

General Staff Responsibilities Appropriate for Staff Members with a Logical–Mathematical Preference

☐ Gather and disaggregate school data for school improvement such as school GPA and discipline statistics
  • Another area would be looking at the data to identify standards and then the specific skills that require improvement on the state assessments
  • Improving state scores in specific areas is discussed in detail in this book in the curriculum development chapter

☐ Determine skills to be developed in the advisory program

☐ Develop calendars weekly and monthly for the school, to include birthdays and other events

☐ Create directional signs for the school

☐ Put together team and/or departmental résumés

☐ Help find patterns of learning connections on curriculum maps to develop interdisciplinary ongoing student projects (see Chapter 7)

☐ Work on the discipline policy

☐ Work on the master schedule

☐ Help develop the team and/or departmental goals

☐ Develop the team and/or departmental self-assessments to evaluate goal achievement
  (I think I should mention that there is a very good teaming assessment in the book Get Fit!*)*

☐ Work on the budget committee

☐ Keep the score books at athletic events

☐ Start a school store

Differentiated Leadership

- [ ] Sponsor clubs and activities of interest such as the math or chess club
- [ ] Help set up and run fundraisers
- [ ] Put together a school map to give to visitors to the school
- [ ] Develop a system of recognitions/rewards for the staff and students

A Specific Project Begging for Staff Members with Logical–Mathematical Talents

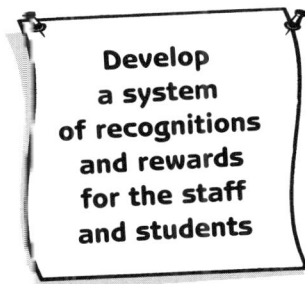

> Develop a system of recognitions and rewards for the staff and students

The administrative team should try to spend at least as much time with positive reinforcements such as reward systems, as they do with the systems of consequences in the building. This is not an easy task to accomplish, but pays off with fewer and fewer needs for the consequence systems. There should be several overlapping reward systems because, as previously discussed, not all reward systems work for all staff members and students.

Remember that rewards perceived as beyond reach by some participants are not perceived as rewards by those people. Later I will share positive reinforcements with proactive student-management strategies that are designed to motivate all students. That means that every student that has a legitimate chance is receiving the award and recognition, and the rewards and recognition are not limited.

Staff members in the logical-mathematical category enjoy designing systems of any kind. When challenged to design reward systems built on a set of criteria that all staff could meet, you would be amazed at what they can come up with. One staff that I work with came up with a set of requirements through which the staff could earn tickets that were entered into drawings at staff meetings, and which could be redeemed after a certain number had been accumulated. The staff established the criteria for earning a ticket, and working with the administrative team, came up with the rewards possible. Again, this is just one of many staff recognition systems this school has in place. It should come as little wonder that the teachers love to teach there, and it should also come as little surprise that they have great test scores!

The following is not a comprehensive list of all the criteria necessary for earning a ticket, but examples include:

- sponsoring a club or organization
- coaching
- after-school tutoring
- before-school tutoring
- attending extracurricular activities
- helping another teacher (one teacher could request tickets for a second teacher based on sharing what the second teacher had done to help the requesting teacher)
- home visiting
- making a certain number of parent/guardian contacts (positive contacts count as two contacts), and so on.

As I mentioned above, the tickets were given out weekly, and the drawings were held every other week at staff meetings

Several staff members helped set up the criteria and the method of documentation. They also had to decide on the distribution method, set up implementation, and so on. Staff members in this category enjoy working on establishing the various criteria, getting documentation methods in place, and putting together methods of distribution. As you will see in the interpersonal intelligence, there are also staff members that enjoy soliciting area businesses for the rewards as well! Yes, there is just something for everyone.

Art Smart

Visual–Spatial

Verbs That Describe Visual–Spatial Behaviors:

design, demonstrate, diagram, expand, graph, identify, illustrate, integrate, interpret, model, observe, organize, and visualize

General Staff Responsibilities Appropriate for Staff Members with a Visual–Spatial Preference

☐ Decorate hallways

☐ Set up displays

☐ Create a video to highlight the school

☐ Help select books and materials to develop the curriculum for the advisory program

- [ ] Help build the COWs for curriculum mapping and integration (pictures at right and below)
- [ ] Help put together the school handbook
- [ ] Help work on the master schedule
- [ ] Help create slide shows with digital pictures to show at events
- [ ] Help create a school Web Site
  - Create a Team Web Site
  - Create a Departmental Web Site
- [ ] Put together informational bulletin boards
- [ ] Create school brochure for
  - Parents
  - The community
- [ ] Sponsor clubs and activities of interest
- [ ] Work on the school landscaping committee
- [ ] Start an Adopt-a-Hallway program
- [ ] Design door name plates
- [ ] Design directional signs for all areas of the school
- [ ] Design certificates for recognizing staff and student achievements.

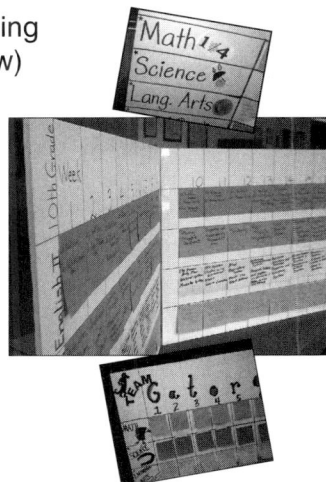

A Specific Project Begging for Staff Members with Visual–Spatial Talents

> Help build
> and use
> the COWs
> for curriculum
> mapping and
> integration

You will learn later about the exact meaning of COWs. For now, it is sufficient that you understand that it is an acronym for a curriculum mapping process. I have found that there are staff members that enjoy building and decorating the curriculum maps much more than the actual curriculum mapping process. In Chapter 7 of this book, "Differentiated Curriculum Development," the administrative team will "see" that this is a very visual process. (It should be noted that this process is also tactile, which goes in the next area, and auditory as the teachers discuss and develop cross-curriculum learning connections).

Body Smart

Body–Kinesthetic

Verbs That Describe Body–Kinesthetic Behaviors:

act out, build, categorize, classify, create, demonstrate, design, document, find, investigate, keep records, locate, perform, produce, search, touch, transfer, and write

General Staff Responsibilities Appropriate for Staff Members with a Body–Kinesthetic Preference

☐ Help set up demonstration days for parents, school board members, etc.

☐ Help study student movement for the most efficient ways to pass students between classes for the master schedule

☐ Help set up "Im-Press" day at school to highlight staff achievements for the local press

☐ Help build and utilize curriculum maps for integrating the various content areas

☐ Help develop and lead staff "team-building" activities

☐ Help set up staff intramurals

☐ Sponsor door or hallway decorating contests

☐ Help put up displays of student work both in the school and in local businesses

☐ Help get together and organize teacher teams for city leagues

☐ Help set up having massages available occasionally at school for the teachers and staff

☐ Administrators visit classrooms often

☐ Help create a staff fitness program

☐ Work with the school beautification committee

☐ Help build and place directional signs for all areas of the school

☐ Help set up a walking nature trail around the school property

☐ Help set up a "Hall Walkers" program for the staff and local seniors

☐ Help decorate the hallways and bulletin boards that are in public areas of the school

A Specific Project Begging for Staff Members with Body–Kinesthetic Talents

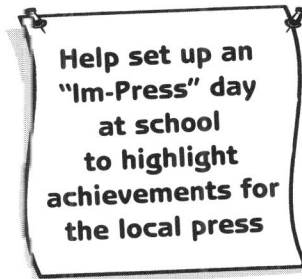

> Help set up an "Im-Press" day at school to highlight achievements for the local press

During my first job as a principal, I was trying to find ways to publicize the great work that the teachers were doing when I came up with "Im-Press" Days. The idea was to invite the local media to the school and hopefully "impress" the press with various projects and positive things we had going on in the school. We invited the local print, radio, and television media to the school for a morning.

The main trick for success is to give the media plenty of lead time, and constantly remind them of the upcoming "Im-Press" Day. The administrative team will want to work with the staff to have stations set up to demonstrate student and staff achievements. Be sure to have a couple of opportunities for the press to visit classrooms and see lessons in progress. Just as I am demonstrating in this chapter, have a variety of "experiences" for the press.

You need to anticipate that regardless of what you tell them, different press people will show up at different times. We had student groups that welcomed various press representatives as they arrived, taking them for an orientation tour and then on to the various activities we had set up for the press to take part in. I was pleasantly surprised by the willing involvement of staff members who wanted to help set the day up as well as by others who volunteered to mount displays, coach the students, and so forth.

Music Smart

Musical–Rhythmic

Verbs That Describe Musical–Rhythmic Behaviors:
amplify, classify, compose, create, demonstrate, express, hear, illustrate, interpret, listen, perform, present, recognize patterns, and show

General Staff Responsibilities Appropriate for Staff Members with a Musical/Rhythmic Preference

☐ Have music in the teacher's lounge (get the favorite music of each teacher!)

☐ Help set up cafeteria, hallway, main office music, etc.

☐ Help create jingles for the school

☐ Help sponsor songwriting contests to highlight the school

☐ Help set up evening events requiring sound

☐ Help organize and run a staff and/or student and/or parent talent show

☐ Help organize and run a school fundraiser

☐ Help work on the master schedule

☐ Help put together skits for parent nights or student demonstrations (such as demonstrating the dress code)

☐ Create a staff fitness program (like jazzercise)

☐ Help work with the school beautification committee

☐ Build directional signs for all areas of the school

☐ Help choreograph the teacher performance at the talent show

☐ Help set up the curriculum maps and work to find core/exploratory learning connections

☐ Help with presentations to the school board and/or parent meetings

☐ Help set up the homecoming activities

A Specific Project Begging for Staff Members with Musical/Rhythmic Talents

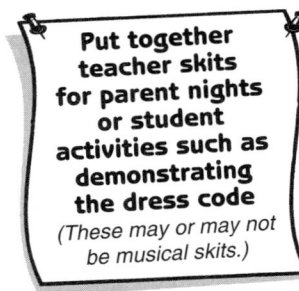

> **Put together teacher skits for parent nights or student activities such as demonstrating the dress code**
> (These may or may not be musical skits.)

Most administrators can relate to this. Some of the most embarrassing, and yet productive, activities for me as an administrator have been when I have participated with other staff members in skits and other "performances" the staff members have choreographed for us to do at various events. I have had many administrators share with me that students or parents will regularly reflect to them, often many years after the fact, that one of these "performances" was one of their most memorable school experiences.

Administrative teams will also see that there are many staff members that will enjoy helping set up these types of events, like talent shows. I am also continually surprised at the staff turnout as spectators at these types of events. Surely it is not because they might enjoy watching the administrative team possibly make fools of themselves! Watch out for those pictures sometime down the road.

People Smart

Interpersonal

Verbs That Describe Interpersonal Behaviors:
advise, associate, brainstorm, coach, compose, demonstrate, discuss, experience, give feedback, interview, listen, motivate, organize, role play, share, and write

General Staff Responsibilities Appropriate for Staff Members with an Interpersonal Preference

- ☐ Work on academies, teams, committees, cross-grade-level houses, magnet programs, etc.
- ☐ Be a team leader and/or department chairperson, etc.
- ☐ Help work on the master schedule
- ☐ Have study groups for the staff for professional development and for personal interest
- ☐ Create team, grade level, or staff résumés
- ☐ Help with the advisory program
- ☐ Set up open houses
- ☐ Contact local businesses to put up displays of student work
- ☐ Help develop business-school partnerships
- ☐ Set up the staff "Fun and Frolic" committee (sometimes also called the social committee) to celebrate staff birthdays and so much more
- ☐ Brainstorm ideas for school improvement

☐ Greet parents and offer a "Valet Service" at open houses

☐ Solicit rewards for staff and students to use the various reward/positive reinforcement systems from local businesses

☐ Work in concession stands at events

☐ Collaborate in curriculum mapping, integrating the curriculums and developing interdisciplinary learning connections

☐ Present at school board meetings and/or parent nights

☐ Help set up fundraisers

☐ Help create positive reinforcement reward systems for the students and the staff

A Specific Project Begging for Staff Members with Interpersonal Talents

Help
with
advisory
programs

Advisory programs can have a tremendous positive effect on student performance in schools. Building effective advisory programs requires a lot of staff input and ownership. Working to define the advisory program and selecting the appropriate activities usually attracts the staff members with strong affective skills since these are the types of activities that are the focus of most advisory programs. The staff members with the best interpersonal skills are the ones that will be most comfortable working with students in an advisory setting.

It must be noted that advisory programs should be skill based, and there is nothing "fluff" about advisory. I like to refer to skills that are taught in advisory as "student skills." Of course, student skills go far beyond study skills, with the goal being to help the students become more motivated, confident, and responsible learners.

I like to have staff members define the skills for advisory by filling in the blanks in the statement "I could teach any student anything, if only the student could or would ____, ____, ____, and . . . . " (Fill in the blanks for as many as are needed.) Every time I do this activity with a staff, I receive many of the same responses: *listen, participate, bring materials to class, be more organized, follow directions, get along with others, not be disruptive, be willing to attempt new things, not give up so easily, be respectful,* and so on. (In the book *Get Fit!* I have this activity described in detail.) This list will be quite large when finished, and will then become the list of the skills that should be the focus of the advisory program. The skills listed here are almost all affective skills.

Most administrators will quickly see that some staff members will be much more comfortable working with students on these kinds of affective skills. That is because some staff members have stronger affective skills than others. Differentiated leadership is about helping staff members build teaching skills, and affective skills are important skills for teaching. What I have found is that all staff members improve their own affective skills as they teach students how to become better students by developing their affective skills.

So some teachers will be quick to help develop and implement an advisory program. Once an advisory program is up and going, all staff members learn and grow with their students as they work together to develop their affective skills. Cognitive learning cannot take place in a state of affective disorder, and while schools are very focused on the cognitive development, they can never get the best results unless they also focus on affective skill development.

Self Smart

Intrapersonal

Verbs That Describe Intrapersonal Behaviors:

analyze, assess, award, compare and contrast, create, critique, demonstrate, evaluate, illustrate, imagine, interpolate, interpret, plan, prepare, reflect, rewrite, share, and validate

---

General Staff Responsibilities Appropriate for Staff Members with an Intrapersonal Preference

☐ Review self-assessments and help make recommendations for school improvement

☐ Review data for disaggregating to determine standards and skills for improvement

☐ Help set up individual recognition programs for students

☐ Create recognition programs for staff members and awards presentations

☐ Use affective/opinion polls to find out how students, teachers, and community members feel about the school

☐ Read, review, and recommend books for professional development and share in book study groups

☐ Set up a chess tournament (and other competitions) for the staff

☐ Help put content on the curriculum maps

☐ Help find multiple learning connections to spiral and thread together to create ongoing student projects

☐ Put together the PowerPoint for the presentation at school board meetings and/or parent nights

☐ Help find and develop curriculum-based business-school partnerships

☐ Help do the setup work for fundraisers

☐ Help build the school calendar, including the calendar for the social committee to celebrate staff birthdays and other significant events

☐ Help set up the criteria and create positive reinforcement reward systems for the students and the staff

A Specific Project Begging for Staff Members with Intrapersonal Talents

> Review data for disaggregating to determine standards and skills for improvement

I have always had staff members that really enjoy reviewing data and creating summaries for sharing with the administrative team and the rest of the staff. I would put out the word that we would be receiving the results back from a survey or assessment, and that I needed a group that would be interested in reviewing the reports, and creating summaries for the rest of us. I found that I never had a shortage of volunteers, and I would even have to rotate the responsibilities to give everyone interested a chance to participate.

I have found that teachers from any and all areas find this task interesting. I think it must fit their personality for looking at the reports, and probably some like being the first to look at information as it is supplied. Also, reviewing data, creating summaries, and making recommendations for the school are important tasks in relation to the success of the school. I would say that participating in any of the activities listed in this chapter helps the staff members feel like they are all important to the school's success.

Nature Smart

Naturalist

Verbs That Describe Naturalist Behaviors:
observe, explore, collect, recognize patterns, draw, sketch, photograph, grow, seek, nurture, build, categorize, examine, as they all relate to nature

General Staff Responsibilities Appropriate for Staff Members with a Naturalist Preference

☐ Work with students to put in a garden area

☐ Help set up nature walk trails around campus labeling trees, foliage, etc.

☐ Help set up recycling opportunities on campus

☐ Help set up "adopt a hallway" or "adopt a portion of the campus" to keep it clean and/or improve as appropriate

☐ Work on energy conservation at school

☐ Work with students and staff to put up bird houses around campus

☐ Work with students and staff to create a "park" on campus

☐ Help set up outdoor areas for the staff to eat, plan, etc.

☐ Help set up outdoor areas for the students to eat, etc.

☐ Help set up an outdoor challenge course for experiential education and teaching team-building, problem-solving, communication, and so on.

☐ Help establish outdoor classroom areas

☐ Help decorate the teachers' lounge and other areas of the school with foliage (real or artificial!)

☐ Help set up bulletin boards highlighting environmental issues

☐ Sponsor clubs and activities of interest

☐ Set up a display of interesting school artifacts

☐ Set up an orienteering course

☐ Put together for parents and the school board presentations of accomplishments gathered from staff and students

☐ Help put together presentations for the parents and school board about the process of learning and the multiple intelligences, etc.

A Specific Project Begging for Staff Members with Naturalist Talents

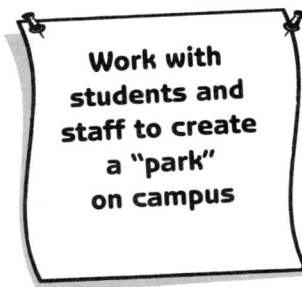

> Work with students and staff to create a "park" on campus

At the last school where I was the principal, a group of teachers and students took this concept even further. They worked with the city and the local power company to have a piece of land near downtown given to them to create their own park, which they would build and maintain. This group created a "Tree Zoo" and planted various species of trees around the "park." They created a mulched walking path and placards to describe what visitors were seeing as they walked through the area.

Now, every year the students and staff not only maintain the park, but also add to it. They have introduced several more species of trees, built an entryway, and constructed a very nice gazebo in the center of the park. Administrators will not have to be told about the many benefits to the school something like this brings. It is a great learning experience for the students and the staff, and the park demonstrates the school's commitment to the community. The public relations generated by the park never ends as people visit or drive by the park at all times. It was encouraging to find that several staff members representing the school put a great deal of time and effort into the park projects.

Conclusion

As the administrative team works with the staff to develop more diverse activities like those listed in this chapter, even more of the staff will become increasingly involved. Because there are activities available to fit the various interests of the staff, the motivation level of the staff also increases. As all staff members get involved with the activities shared here, they impact many others in the school community. The staff will then motivate more students, parents, and community members to become involved in projects and activities linked with the school. Of course, everyone involved also become even more invested in the school. And the good news just keeps getting better!

Differentiated Leadership
Copyright ©2008 by Incentive Publications, Inc., Nashville, TN.

TAG . . . You're It!

Recognizing a Differentiated Staff

Exercise One:

The administrative team should use the examples listed above for each of the activities that correspond to the eight multiple intelligences. The idea of this exercise is to list the activities that staff members have available in your school. Make lists that correlate each of the activities with the appropriate multiple intelligences, and assess where more activities might be needed.

Exercise Two:

Prepare a presentation on the multiple intelligences for the school board and/or a parent night and/or a staff meeting.

_____ Conference Form

Conference: _____ Team/Student _____ Team/Parent _____ Team/Student/Parent

Student's Name: _____ Date: _____

Faculty Present: _____

_____

_____

Areas needing improvement: _____

_____

Content Area Analysis by Individual Teachers:

Read/Write: _____

_____

_____

Math: _____

_____

_____

Science: _____

_____

_____

Social Studies: _____

_____

_____

Other: _____

_____

_____

Recommended adjustments to enhance student performance/achievement:

1. _____

_____

2. _____

_____

3. _____

_____

4. _____

_____

5. _____

_____

Follow-up visit: ___ yes ___ no   Date scheduled: _____

Parent/Guardian Signature/Date: _____

Student Signature/Date: _____

Differentiated Curriculum Development

Chapter 7

Developing Symphonic Curriculums

One of the best metaphors for differentiated leadership comes to life when school leaders become *symphony conductors*. Each of the musicians in a symphony is capable of creating excellent music. But when they play in collaboration with other musicians, the individual sounds blend to create a musical masterpiece. School administrators have to know the strengths of all their staff members, and direct them in a way that blends their various strengths to maximize their performances and create a masterpiece.

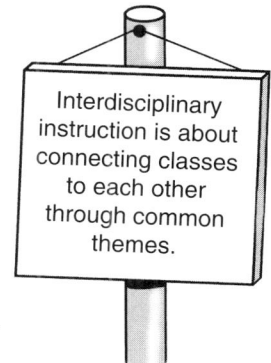

Interdisciplinary instruction is about connecting classes to each other through common themes.

One aspect of differentiated leadership is getting the staff members to recognize and utilize each other's strengths. The task is to find ways to get teachers invested in each other's success, and in this case, work with each other to develop and share curriculum. *(One of the best ways I have found is by getting the teachers together in different combinations to develop curriculum together.)*

Previously, teachers may have developed curriculum in departments. We do need the teachers to work within their departments to ensure the highest level of expertise in each area. Differentiated leadership means creating systems which enable and encourage the various members of the staff to collaborate across content areas to share specific strategies and activities in a way that also promotes individual professional growth. In this model, you will see how to get the teachers from the various departments in your school to work together to develop curriculum across content areas. They will share ideas across content lines regarding specific skills and standards as they apply in the various content areas.

The analogy between a symphony conductor and school administrator is a good one, and it is especially true when leading teachers to integrate the diverse curriculums in the school. The conductor knows when various musicians will enhance the sounds of the other musicians and when a musician will sound best playing solo in relation to the whole symphony. To develop an integrated curriculum, the various subjects in a school must be treated like the musicians in a symphony. The administrators have to help their teachers know when a subject stands best alone, when to tie one subject into another, and when perhaps even several subjects will tie into each other.

Differentiated leadership means that as we develop curriculum we think in much the same way as the composer. In this chapter, I am going to give curriculum leaders the format and the tools to create symphonic curriculums. I will demonstrate for you how to find where the connections between the various content areas of the curriculums happen naturally. Unlike previous interdisciplinary unit methods of integrating the curriculum, teachers will never have to force a connection to relate their subject to an arbitrary theme.

The best tools I have found to help teachers find ways their different subjects relate to one another are affectionately known as COWs. More on that name later, but the COWs represent the simplest way I have found to create easy-to-use, interactive curriculum maps. This process enables administrators to demonstrate for teachers how to communicate with each other about what is going on in each of their classes. Use the process to continue the ongoing alignment of each curriculum area with the state standards; while, at the same time, working to find and develop real and relevant learning connections between subjects. So the purpose of this process is to enable leaders to help teachers find and develop learning connections.

A learning connection is simply the opportunity created when any skills taught in one content area are also used in another content area.

I am going to share an easy-to-implement and user-friendly process for teachers to find these opportunities and then work together to expand and develop the skills that cross the curriculum areas. It is also exciting to see differentiated instruction develop as a natural by-product of this process.

Administrators must be concerned with student performance on the high-stakes tests. Leaders and teachers will learn to use this simple process to cross-reference the standards between content areas. As we go through the process, you will see how to tie the actual test items (released for practice) into the curriculum maps. Through the integration process, teachers in all areas, including related arts, will write test items as a part of their instruction and assessments.

The curriculum maps (COWs) also make it easier for leaders to track and document how effectively programs such as technology and writing across the curriculum are being implemented, and how common resources like the media center are being used. While this process makes integrating the curriculum painless, administrators will also use it to help the departments as they develop their individual curriculum areas.

Using this mapping process, administrators will be able to quickly identify gaps in curriculum areas where standards are not being addressed adequately or, in some cases, not at all. They will also be able to easily identify duplication of the standards and be better able to make decisions about curriculum compacting. Departments will actually be able to do a quick item analysis for state test sample questions.

Using this process, administrators can help teachers develop a more project-based curriculum and smoother transitions between grade levels. The power of this process is in the incredible level of collaboration it creates between teachers, and the multi-layered approach it creates for ensuring student mastery of the state standards. This is the most differentiated way to develop curriculum.

Following the Involvement Model of Change, the first step is to build interest in the process. *(Every time I share this process I find that teachers are very interested because the process is built on each teacher's own curriculum and the students he or she teaches.)* I will give administrators the information that they will need to share with staff. As administrators have teachers share their curriculums in this process, they will get the needed input from the staff about their readiness for developing learning connections. Later, you will see how interest, information, and input continually cycle through this process which makes the implementation almost self-perpetuating.

Finally, I will demonstrate how administrators can use the maps to create unprecedented levels of community involvement in the school. The maps are important components of COMPASS (Community Partnerships Assuring Student Success), a partnership program with businesses and community groups based on the curriculum.

The COWs are key to lifting curriculum collaboration to heights you may not have considered.

This process is discussed from the teacher's perspective in the book Get Fit! The process does not require academies or teams, which is why it works well at both the middle- and high-school levels. However, I do also reference how this process works in academies and teams. The discussion is the same regardless of the term used. To simplify things, I will use the term "team" to mean either team or academy.

Curriculum Mapping
Five Tasks for COWs

1. **Build the COWs by grade level**
   a. Teachers indicate what is taught in each subject area in a weekly outline format
   b. Build the maps by teams, if applicable
   c. Build an exploratory map for each grade level
   d. Indicate state standards and test items on the maps
   e. Indicate media center use, technology implementation, writing programs, etc.

2. **Realign the instructional timelines and agree on curriculum as needed within departments**
   a. Teachers add and delete content as needed
   b. Teachers agree on common instruction and assessments
   c. Add sample state test questions to maps for documentation and use in instruction and assessments

3. **Find learning connections across curriculum areas**
   a. Look for topics that relate, and specific skills that will be used across curriculum areas

4. **Discuss and develop learning connections**
   a. Discuss, develop, and share reference points, activities, extra credit projects, PowerPoint slides, overheads, worksheets, assignments, and assessment items

5. **COMPASS—**
   Community Partnerships Assuring Student Success
   a. Develop a community-based curriculum
   b. Use the COWs as a communication tool to facilitate business partnerships that will help develop and support instruction

Build It and They Will Come

The first step in the process for administrators is to have teachers build the curriculum maps. *(Consider hiring a consultant to train the teachers in building and using the maps.)* The process is very simple and nonintrusive for teachers. They already spend untold hours of time planning for their classes. Instead of adding to the workload, this process takes advantage of the planning that has already taken place to get the curriculum maps ready. The result is a physically and visually interactive version of their existing curriculum. The curriculum maps reflect in the simplest way possible what is currently being taught.

These maps are often called COWs—*COW* stands for *Curriculum On the Wall*. Administrators will appreciate that this acronym comes from a curriculum development workshop where the curriculums were being displayed via overhead projector on a wall. Some of the participants thought we needed a name for these maps and the process, and since the curriculum maps were being projected onto the wall, COW seemed to be as appropriate as anything else. This acronym actually has nothing to do with the process, but it has stuck and is now commonly used to refer to this particular method of curriculum mapping.

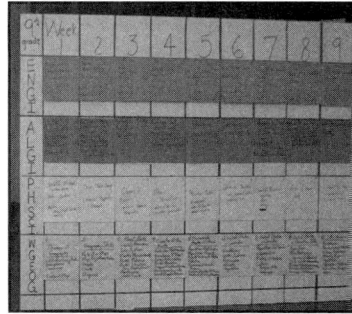

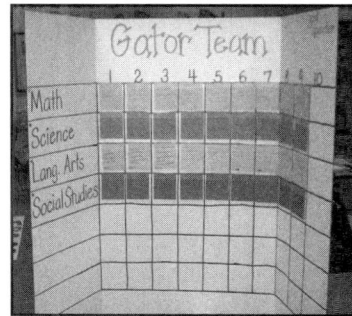

*P*lease notice as you go through this chapter that many schools really play up the COW acronym and have a lot of fun with it! Leaders have come up with things like: calves (a portion of a map); the corral (the room where they work on the maps); and cow brands (the logos used on each map). You get the idea! Although these maps are often displayed on the wall for curriculum development during the week, parent nights, and business partnership meetings, I do not necessarily recommend that they stay on permanent display. The main reason is that most schools simply do not have the extra wall space to keep the maps on permanent display. It is really up to the individual school.

Administrators will need to plan where the maps will be housed and used. Teachers will be attaching adhesive notes, test items, and a variety of other notes to these boards. Therefore, if schools do not have the wall space for a permanent display in a teacher workroom, I recommend that schools keep them folded up in a poster board storage bin when not in use. Even in schools with the wall space available, administrators should consider taking the maps down over holidays and over the summer to fold them flat. This keeps the various items we tape to the boards nice and pressed looking. Otherwise, items attached to the board start to flip up or become unattached because of humidity and, eventually, age.

Find a central area for the maps to be stored where they are easily accessible to everyone who might use them. Some schools have a curriculum development room dedicated for the maps. Others will use teacher work areas such as academy or team areas or departmental areas for the maps. The maps will not be used if they are difficult to get to and use. Leaders are going to want these maps to be used weekly and by multiple teachers and support personnel from multiple content areas.

Let the staff know that the idea is for these maps to be used indefinitely. The pictures that follow show COWs in the early stages. *(I guess you could call these calves.)* Provide the materials needed for the staff. Various types of poster boards can be used for this project. The basic materials needed include: various colors of adhesive notes, pens, scissors, tape, and the poster boards. *(As you see, this is a very low-tech operation!)*

COW Tools

You may want to have the poster boards ready for the teachers to use right away. On the poster boards, draw squares slightly larger than the size of a regular adhesive note. Label the grid. List the subjects down the left side, and number weeks across the top. Each column will represent one week of curriculum in each subject area.

Leaders will want teachers in each subject to use a different-colored adhesive note. This will help the teachers as they use the maps but, as you will see, color-coding will be of great assistance to administrators for documentation and accountability purposes. For example, math might use blue adhesive notes, language arts might use yellow, social studies might use orange, and of course, science would use green. Each elective/related arts/exploratory class should also have its own color. You will not be able to tell in the grayscale pictures, but the maps are color coded so that we know what subject each color represents.

If you do not have teams in your building, then one core map for each grade level will do. However, if you have teams in your school, then I recommend that every team in the building should have its own map. This will allow leaders to work with each team individually to develop connections and units without being locked into each other. It will be important for leaders to create a time once a month or so for the teams to share learning connections they are working on with the other teams at their grade level.

Administrators should not try to get all of the teams at a grade level implementing the exact same learning connections or instructional units that any of the other teams are doing. However, there are several benefits to the teams sharing what curriculum connections they have found. First, no team wants to come to the sharing time with nothing to share! No team worth their salt wants to be outdone by the other teams; and, if this is handled correctly by the administrative team, this can provide additional motivation. You also want to encourage sharing simply so that we are not re-inventing the same wheel over and over.

Differentiated leadership implies that leaders promote collaboration across content lines, and this process is the perfect way for administrators to get the elective teachers working with the core teachers in a meaningful way. The elective team should create one curriculum map for each grade level. Each grade level elective curriculum map will show the elective classes available for that grade level. Most elective classes are available at each grade level. Even if some elective classes are really doing the same thing in more than one grade level, that elective teacher should duplicate the subject on each grade level curriculum map.

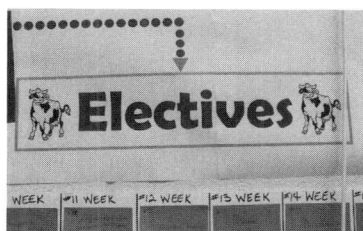

When administrators are working with the elective teachers it is helpful to remember that sometimes there are cross-grade-level elective classes, like band. Even though this band class is the same for two or more grade levels, it still should be written on each individual grade level curriculum map. Semester classes do not have to be written twice. Just number the weeks to indicate that the weeks are repeated in the second semester. So Week 1 will have Week 1 and Week 19, Week 2 will have Week 2 and Week 20, and so on. This will indicate that Week 1 in art will be repeated in Week 19.

The curriculum leaders will need to demonstrate to teachers how to fill out the adhesive notes that they will be attaching to the COWs. Encourage teachers to use a different color adhesive note for each subject. As we have listed earlier, for example, math might use blue notes, language arts might use yellow, social studies might use orange, and of course, science could use green. Each elective/related arts/exploratory class should also have its own color.

Each adhesive note represents one week of curriculum in each area. Include three pieces of information on each adhesive note.

1) *The number of the week*
(If an adhesive note falls off, it will be easy to put it back in the correct spot.) The number of the week is not set in stone. Teams and schools build the maps once, then adjust them as needed. If a teacher reaches a topic a couple of weeks earlier or later over the year, the map does not need to be changed.

2) *Content taught*
Be as generic as possible when describing what is being taught. State the topic succinctly—the fewer words used, the better. (*A good tip: write large! Writing large on small piece of paper limits the amount that can be written. Also, the large print is so much easier to read.*) Do not include any description of instructional strategies or methodologies; give only an overall topic for what is taught. The more generic the title or topic, the more useful the map will be. If something is taught for several weeks, repeat the title as needed. For example, *Civil War* may be written in several weeks if needed.

3) *The state standard that is addressed by the week's topic*
Most often, more than one standard is being taught, so all standards that might be covered by that topic should be listed. Use the numbers and letters that represent the standards, and do not write out the standards, as they are often quite lengthy.

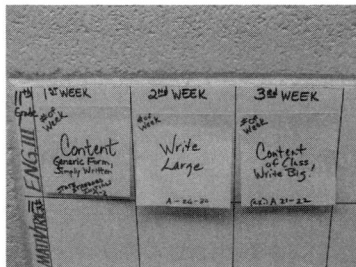

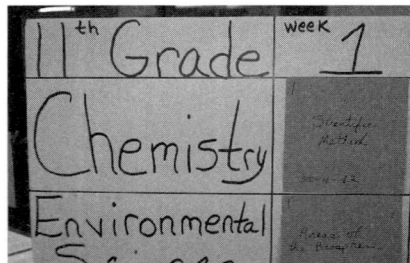

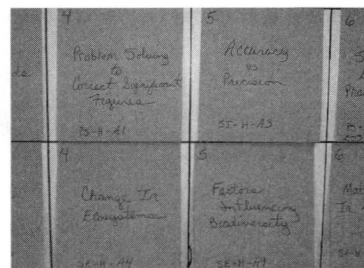

Middle-school and high-school examples of curriculum maps

Differentiated Leadership

What Are We Currently Teaching?

Of course, the first task of the process is to get the maps built. Teachers are to fill in the adhesive notes based on what they have done in the past. *(In curriculum workshops, I have teachers use their last year's plan books and/or the district curriculum pacing guide to fill in the adhesive notes. It is important that the administrative team keep the task of building the maps easy because you want to build on the planning that has already been done.)* It is important for leaders to know what is actually being taught in the current curriculums—and work from there. The maps are going to be used to plan for the future but, for the task of building the maps, we use what has already been done.

Ensuring Alignment with State Standards

Administrators know that after taking the high-stakes tests, students often come back and say things like "the teachers didn't teach us some of that stuff." Of course, this is not what educators want to hear—especially since leaders and teachers worked so hard to make sure that all of the standards are being addressed in each area. However, when leaders and teachers look at individual test items, they can see the problem. Teachers may very well have covered the topic, but for some of the standards the assessments did not ask the kinds of questions that the state asks. The interpretation of the standard can vary and often teacher-created test questions are worded differently than questions on the standardized tests.

With the COWs, this is a problem that is easily solved. First, accumulate all of the released and sample items for the state standards. These are most often available on the State Department of Education websites. Then cut the sample test items so that individual test items on on separate strips of paper. Work with each team. Have the teachers look at each test item, read it aloud, and ask, "When would I ask this question?" Then the assessment item is folded and taped to the board under the appropriate week.

As the administrative team, you should expect questions to fall into three categories:

1) Questions that are currently in use
The department knows exactly where the state questions fit into their curriculum, and they ask that kind of question often. It is pretty easy to see why these tend to also be the ones the students are most successful with.

2) Questions that assess skills that are taught, but are not being asked
Sometimes, these are also the questions the staff knows should be on the board, but they are not quite sure which area to put them in. These questions may combine concepts or use wording that might mislead students, but they are the ones where the staff sees where students might get confused. Here is where the leaders and the teachers have to decide how to clarify the questions for the students.

3) Questions that simply do not fit on the COWs
In other words, the teachers do not ask this question at all; it is not currently contained in their curriculum. Sometimes teachers will argue that these items do not fit what they thought the corresponding state standard meant, and it is a matter of interpretation. Other times each grade thinks one of the other grades is covering this topic, and it actually is not being covered by anyone. Needless to say, students generally do not perform very well on test items they have never seen before.

*E*very school that I have worked with has had items fall into all three categories when they look at the test items one at a time. I ask teachers to look at each

*of the released test items and determine when that
particular question would be asked. I very often hear,
"I do not ask that particular question," or "I would not
have asked that question in that way." Every teacher-
constructed test should not look just like the state test
by any means, but every state question should be a part
of the instruction and assessment process the teachers
will use for each unit of instruction.*

After the teachers have placed the sample assessment items on
the curriculum maps, they will make copies of the assessment items
for each instructional unit. Curriculum leaders and teachers should
use these assessment items, along with the ones already developed
for the unit, to drive the planning for each instructional unit.
Administrators should make sure that teachers are checking for new
state sample assessment items every year, and that they are adding
any new items to the maps.

This is a very visual process, and if there happen to be any gaps in
the curriculums, they are easy to see. Weeks where there are no test
items attached to the map indicate that what is being taught those
weeks is not assessed by the state proficiency tests. That does not
mean the content in those areas is not important or that it should
not be taught. However, if there are several weeks in any content
area where there are no released questions attached, leaders will
want to work with the department to look at what the curriculum
priorities are going to be.

The administrative team and the departments may want to reduce
the amount of time spent on areas that are not tested, and put some
of that effort into the "category two questions" (those that are
confusing), and the "category three questions" (those that are not
being covered at all). Having the curriculum maps will give leaders
and teachers an easy way to do an item analysis on all of the sample
state test items that are available. This process is easily the most
effective way to make use of the sample state test items. In the
pictures below, the folded slips of paper are individual sample state
test items that have been attached to the COWs.

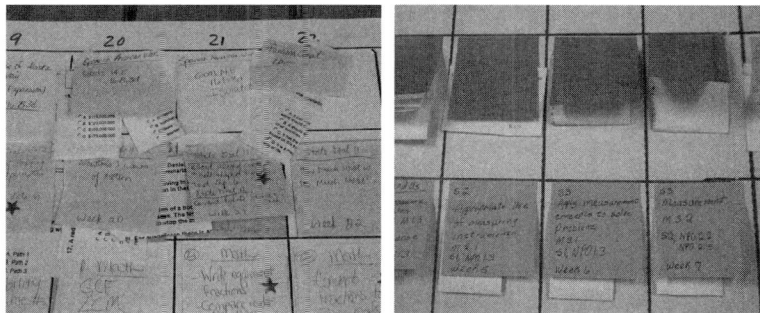

Using the COWs to Track and Document Programs

The administrative team can also use the maps to track other important areas. For example, leaders can have teachers use the small sticky dots (the type available at office supply stores that are used for filing and categorizing) to track things like the use of technology, writing programs, community partnerships, and the media center. In one school, the teachers use blue sticky dots to indicate the use of technology in their classes. First, their administrative team along with their teachers had to determine what was included in the use of technology. *(And they decided not to count showing videos.)* Then each teacher simply puts a blue dot on any week where he or she uses technology as a part of their instruction and assessment.

The technology coordinators for the school or district can look at the maps and quickly see where technology is already being utilized successfully. They can then provide support for teachers more effectively and efficiently. For example, as new software applications become available, technology coordinators know where the software can be best used. They can schedule computer time more efficiently. Technology coordinators will see the gaps in the use of technology within the building. If there are no blue dots in a content area, the coordinators can help teachers apply technology. It becomes very easy to see which staff members might need a little more assistance with training or the implementation of technology.

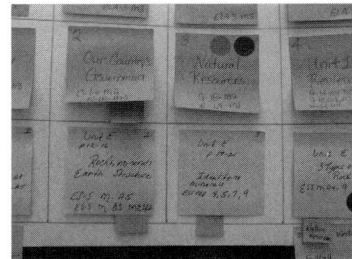

Another area administrative teams like to focus on is the use of the media center. This same school has the teachers put a red dot in any week where they used the media center as a part of their instruction. Again, the administrative team and teachers had to discuss what they were going to consider as the actual use of the media center. For example, they decided that teachers occasionally letting students go to the media center to return books would not be considered using the media center as part of instruction. When the administrative team saw that there were several areas that did not have a single red dot on their subject row, they could then work with the media specialist to target support.

With this visual process, anyone can tell at a glance what colors are included in what rows, and of course, what colors are not included in some subjects. That gives the administrative team, media specialists, and technology coordinators much needed information, and this allows them to be more proactive and productive. Media specialists and technology specialists can look at areas where there is no or little use, look at the topics, and make specific suggestions to those teachers for the use of technology or the media center. Of course, this also allows the media and technology specialists to plan well in advance for impending projects.

The administrative team and teachers can also use the dots and maps to build their community partnership program. This will be discussed in detail in the next chapter. The administrative team will share the maps with various businesses and community groups. Ask them to indicate with a dot, star, or adhesive note any topics that fit into their area of expertise. This program is called COMPASS, which stands for Community Partnerships Assuring Student Success.

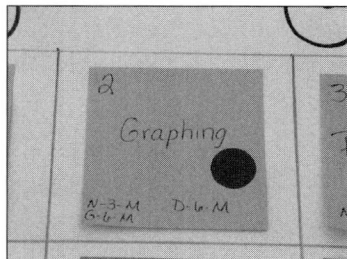

Connecting The Dots—Finding Learning Connections

The expectation of the administrative team should be that teachers use the maps for a few minutes every week. Each week, every teacher should be doing one or both of two things. On a weekly basis, each teacher should be using the maps to find a learning connection, or develop one they have identified previously. If your school has interdisciplinary teams, the teams should make curriculum development a weekly, prescheduled team meeting topic. This process should also be a topic at every department meeting.

The administrative team should lead in this process. There should be an established time and place for teams, departments, and individuals to work on the COWs. This way the leaders will know when to be present to support this process. Teachers are much more likely to participate if they know the administrative team will be participating as well. Whether working with a team, a department, or alone, the teachers should look at curriculum areas besides their own. When they look at another curriculum area, they are to look for a key word or phrase that matches a skill they teach in their own area.

LEARNING CONNECTIONS—any time a teacher finds that a skill taught in his or her content area is also used in another content area. When teachers identify *learning connections*, then they work together to develop and demonstrate the application of the skill in both areas.

The administrative team will want to support teachers in looking for learning connections. For example, the math teacher might look for places where charts and graphs might be applied. This could lead to a discussion with the social studies teacher as they look at how charts and graphs are used in the social studies unit on elections. In fact, the math teacher will undoubtedly find numerous places where charts and graphs could be used in other subjects. The math teacher will want to look for every opportunity for the application of charts and graphs throughout the various core classes and encore classes. This could happen dozens of times.

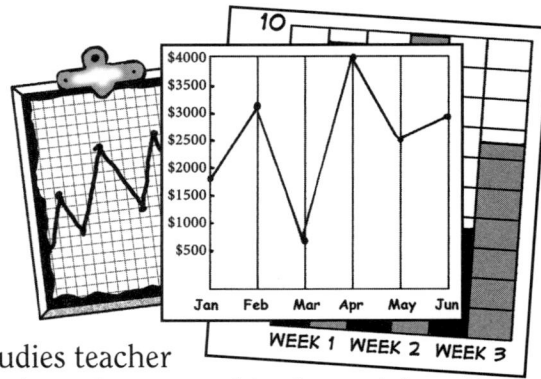

The administrative team might want teachers to focus first on finding learning connections with skills in areas that are targeted for improvement. The leaders will want to disaggregate test score data and share with teachers what specific standards and skills teachers might want to focus on initially. As teachers develop learning connections, students' comprehension and retention of the skills improve. That is why many schools will begin by targeting certain standards and skills.

The administrative team can alleviate much of the stress that is often associated with an integrated approach to developing curriculum. Since there will almost always be multiple connections for any skill that the teachers will be developing, the timing for learning connections will only occasionally happen simultaneously. It is important for leaders and teachers to understand that most learning connections will actually happen over time. It is much more likely that learning connections will happen over extended periods of time. If we do not limit ourselves to concurrent learning connections, the number of learning connections is unlimited.

It is a misconception that interdisciplinary instruction means that everyone will be doing the same "theme" at the same time. I am going to demonstrate how to develop learning connections over time. That way, teachers do not ever have to change the order and timing of their subject to coincide with another teacher if it does not fit the natural flow of their subject.

A great example for leaders is the use of "guided choice" assignments. For example, the language arts teacher might look for topics from other areas when she begins the unit on descriptive paragraphs. After teaching about descriptive paragraphs, she might give students "guided choices" for writing their descriptive paragraphs. These "choices" will come from things they have already studied, like polygons or molecules. Or she might do the k-part of the k-w-l for one of the other teachers by having students describe something they are going to be studying later in one of the other subjects. So the students are going to choose to write about things they have already studied or will be studying.

When a teacher sees a topic in another area that uses skills from his area, he should indicate that learning connection on the maps. The teacher will either use full-size adhesive notes or one of the tabs, and he will write the skill, the week it is from, and the state standards associated with that skill on the new adhesive notes. Then the teacher will attach the adhesive notes to the other teachers' row where the connection is going to occur. He will lift up the other teachers' adhesive notes and place his underneath indicating the possible connection. Any time teachers see other adhesive notes, they know that another teacher is indicating that there might be a learning connection between their two areas. *(Different-colored notes make these connections easy to see.)*

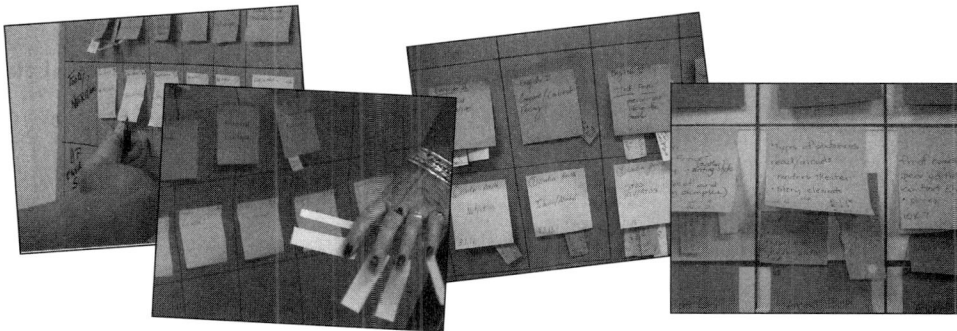

Developing Learning Connections

Basically the maps become big "notepads" for the teachers to write notes to each other indicating an interest in that topic. Once teachers have found learning connections, the next task is to discuss and develop those learning connections. The following is a list of some of the possibilities for teachers to consider when developing learning connections.

The maps are also then available for the administrative team, specialists, district level curriculum personnel, and even community members to review what is being taught and how they might best be able to support the instruction. Participation is easily documented by counting the appropriate color of tab or dot to see how often learning connections are being developed. (Page 174 is a simple form for teachers to fill out for each learning connection.) Leaders will want to use the following list as a reference and check list to see what types of learning connections the teachers are working on.

Developing Learning Connections

When developing learning connections, teachers should consider different levels of connections. (Details for each level are described on pages 156 through 170.)

1. **Refer to the use of the same skill in both classes.**
   Teachers connect skills in one class to specific topics and times in other classes. So a teacher tells students specifically when and where the skills they are learning will be used in other classes.

2. **Share demonstration materials.**
   Teachers share resources that are appropriate in both classes (overheads, PowerPoint slides, supplemental resources).

3. **Share instructional activities.**
   Teachers use the same worksheets in both classes. Students complete part of the worksheet in one class and the remainder of the worksheet in another class.

4. **Give students guided choice assignments.**
   For example, the language arts teacher gives students writing choices with the topics selected from content in other classes.

5. **Give students extra credit for the work done in another teacher's class.**
   The value and relevancy of work goes up for students when they receive credit for the work from more than one teacher.

6. **Share assessment items.**
   Assessment items from each area should show up on multiple assessments in multiple content areas.

7. **Save and share student work to develop embedded themes and ongoing projects.**
   Combinations of learning connections will lead to recurring embedded themes and ongoing projects. Saving student work will require the teachers to assist students in maintaining portfolios.

Differentiated Leadership
Copyright ©2008 by Incentive Publications, Inc., Nashville, TN.

Timing Is Not Everything!

Learning connections may happen concurrently. Teachers may be able to develop and implement the learning connection and coordinate activities at the same time. For example, the language arts teacher may teach how to use the Internet for research at the same time the social studies teacher is having students investigate a famous black American for Black History Month. So the two teachers work together on the project, and the students get two grades on the one project—one for language arts and one for social studies.

Many teachers consider only concurrent connections when they are thinking about learning connections. It is important to note that only occasionally will the timing of skills being taught in one content area line up nicely with what is happening in another content area. Because of that, teachers may feel they need to change the sequence of their lessons to align with the content of the other area, whether it fits the flow of their class or not. Or even worse, all of the teachers on the team are told that they have to tie their subjects into one theme all at the same time, regardless of whether or not it is timely for their subject. *(This should never happen.)*

A teacher should never be forced to adapt his or her curriculum to another teacher's curriculum if it does not naturally fit with the flow of the class at the time. *(Later in this chapter, I will demonstrate how to develop themes in the more appropriate, natural way.)* It is much more likely that learning connections will happen over extended periods of time. If we do not limit ourselves to concurrent learning connections, the number of learning connections is unlimited.

Imagine learning connections that happen over an extended period of time. Although a skill taught in one area may not be used in another area for weeks or even months, the skill will probably be used in multiple areas many times throughout the year. The number of possibilities for these extended learning connections is endless. One teacher can be referencing something in another teacher's class that is not going to happen for many weeks or even months. (The learning connections become *distributed practice*.)

When teachers look for learning connections that happen over an extended period of time, they can also begin to develop ongoing projects that grow throughout the school year. Students develop portfolios to hold developing projects that require different work from each of the subject areas during the year. Interdisciplinary units (IDUs) are powerful and motivating for students, but it's a terrible waste to develop only connections that happen in the same week or two in a traditional interdisciplinary unit.

For example, the math teacher may see that the social studies teacher teaches a unit on elections, and the math teacher is about to teach a unit on charts and graphs. The problem is that the social studies teacher does not teach the elections unit until weeks 28 through 30, and the math teacher plans to teach charts and graphs in weeks 8 through 10. It is important that both teachers teach their content in the appropriate sequence. Do not ask the social studies teacher to move the unit to weeks 8 through 10 to match the math sequence, but create a powerful connection anyway.

As leaders work with the teachers, here is an example of how the discussion should happen. The math teacher should ask the social studies teacher if charts and graphs are important to the elections unit. The social studies teacher gives the math teacher examples of charts and graphs from the social studies book, along with worksheets and assessments used during an elections unit in the social studies class. *(Electronic files are particularly helpful!)*

The math teacher copies the materials. Then the math teacher does a little "cutting and pasting" and has new worksheets to use with the charts and graphs unit. The students are blown away by the fact that each one of the examples on the new worksheets comes directly from their social studies book and class materials.

More Relevance By Having Teachers Reference One Class in Another

Often students ask, "When are we ever going to use this stuff again?" Now the math teacher can say, "In 20 weeks and two days, you will use these very same problems in the social studies class." The math teacher can even reference the chapter and page numbers in the social studies book. In addition, the social studies teacher might suggest that the math teacher put an opinion question on each of the worksheets to get student opinions and knowledge about the election process. The students get credit in math for giving their opinions about elections, while the social studies teacher gets valuable information to use for planning for the elections unit later in the year.

Teachers Share Instructional Materials and Activities

When the math teacher finishes the unit, the completed worksheets are given to the social studies teacher to hold until the elections unit. During the elections unit, the social studies teacher will have the students use their math work to help them complete their social studies assignments. The students think it is great to already have some of the answers, and the teachers know it is great to have the students revisiting the math work. The social studies teacher asks students to revise their responses to the opinion questions as they go through the elections unit. *(Often students do not like to be involved with revisions; however, these revisions are different because the original assignment is for another teacher.)*

Another example of a learning connection is developed between the art teacher and the math teacher. The art teacher notices the phrase "line design" in the math teacher's row. The art teacher attaches a note with the words "string art" on it. The math teacher has no clue what string art is. When the art teacher and the math teacher meet, the math teacher learns that string art is a physical representation of a line design created on boards using nails or pegs and a variety of textures of string such as fishing line and yarn. Now the math teacher uses the string art as a portion of the assessment rubric for his unit on line design. All math students rotate through the art class during the school year. As the math students rotate through the art class, the math teacher will give the students points for completed string art projects done in art class. The art teacher uses the line designs generated in math as the templates for students to use in art, and the art and math grades become interdependent.

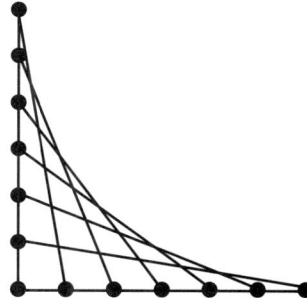

State standards are involved in each of the examples. The social studies teacher references sample questions to see how questions for charts and graphs will look on the math portion of the state test. The math teacher will have examples of social studies questions, and the two teachers will reinforce each other's curriculum. The math teacher can share with the art teacher the types of questions asked regarding angle classification and measurement, and specifically how they are worded. When all teachers share their assessments, students see some of the same assessment items on multiple assessments in multiple areas.

Offer Guided Choice Assignments and Extra Credit

Guided choice assignments are powerful because students feel more ownership since they have some choice in the work they do. For example, the language arts teacher has been teaching the students about descriptive writing and is ready to have the students actually do some writing for evaluation.

The language arts teacher gives the students several choices developed from the COWs and team planning. The students may choose to write descriptive paragraphs about topics such as molecules, polygons, biomes, the Internet, sculpture, and music composition. The language arts teacher includes two possibilities from each of the subjects that the students are taking.

The writing task and the skills are the same regardless of the topic chosen, and yet, the students will report every time that they are going to write about the "easy" one. Of course, learning preferences play a big role in the students' choices, and a student's interest level in the writing improves with the element of choice. Guided choices provide relevancy to both subjects involved.

Students will also become more invested in the assignment if extra credit is available. The team may decide that any time a student participates in work in one class that relates to another, the second teacher will give the student extra credit. To receive credit, students show the completed assignment to the second teacher. The assignment now carries grade value in two classes. Two teachers are encouraging students to complete the assignment, and to do it well.

Learning Connections Become Embedded Themes, Ongoing Projects, and Often Yearlong Projects

One social studies teacher developed a learning connection with a science teacher. They connected the local history of their area and an environmental unit. Since logging was a major part of the local history, the social studies teacher recognized a natural connection with the study of the rainforest that was a part of a science environmental unit. The science teacher taught the environmental unit a few months before the social studies teacher introduced the local history. The social studies teacher required students to compare and contrast what is happening to the rainforest today with how logging evolved in their area, in the United States, and around the world.

In science, the students visited previously logged sites to see the environmental impact, and to view the reforestation process. The students also visited a museum and sawmill to see how the logging industry had evolved, and to observe its impact. Several pieces of work from the environmental unit provided a starting point for work in the history unit. The two teachers gave the students extra credit for each piece of science that related to social studies, and vice versa.

Meanwhile, within the same team, the language arts teacher developed a learning connection with the math teacher. The math teacher put students in five-person "construction companies" and gave students directions for building three different decks. (She got the plans from a local lumberyard.) Students were given this scenario:

> *A new subdivision is being built with several hundred new homes. Each home will include one of the three decks. Your construction company would like to build all of the decks. Prepare a bid for the job, giving a detailed line-item cost analysis.*

The language arts teacher saw a potential learning connection. During a unit on business letter writing, students could write a cover letter for the bid. The math teacher taught the bid unit first, and saved the student work. Several weeks later, the language arts teacher took the bids and helped students organize the information and write professional cover letters.

A Real-world Connection

One year, during this unit, the science teacher was actually building a deck at his home, which was located a few blocks from the school. Several of the bus routes passed near the science teacher's home, and the students started pressing the science teacher for information about his deck to try to get the inside track on their bids. One of the student teams asked to visit the project at the science teacher's house. The science teacher agreed to let the students visit, and was proud to show his handiwork and answer their questions. Two of the girls in the groups were looking at his directions and some of the boards he had precut to show the students, and they were happy to let him know that he had cut them incorrectly according to the schematic he was working from. The embarrassed science teacher quickly replied, "I meant to do it that way." Improvising, he said, "See that small oak tree? As you can see, the deck is going to go past the oak tree, so I have cut these boards shorter to allow room for the tree. It is a small oak tree now, but I want to leave room for it when it grows."

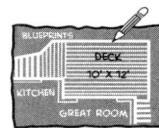

Hearing this, one of the boys in the group asked, "Why don't you just cut down the oak tree?" Like any good steward of the environment, the science teacher was worried about this response and asked why the students would even consider such a thing.

Another student replied, "You see, we're businessmen now. Our company is going to buy the materials, precut them, and store them by design. All we have to do is pick up the materials, go to the site, and put the deck together. If we were to have to change the design, it would take more time and then cost us more. When you own your own company, time is money!"

Needless to say, the science teacher was not impressed with time and money taking priority over the environment. So he asked the students, "What is your company's environmental policy?" The students said, quite matter-of-factly, that an environmental policy was not part of the assignment; their only concern was to determine how much they were going to charge to build each of the decks. *(Given the nature of this chapter, I am sure you already know what happened next.)* The science teacher was not going to let this go on, and another project was born.

A project which began in math with an interesting assignment to bid on an imagined construction project moved numerous times through the language arts curriculum. The science teacher added the task of writing an environmental policy. The students became environmental specialists for their construction companies. They had to determine what the environmental issues might be with construction projects. For practice, they did an environmental impact study of the school to determine where decks might be best added for outside activities at the school. The students saved their policies in portfolios with their previous work.

Portfolio Records

Interdisciplinary projects require the development of portfolio records. In the construction company scenario, students worked with the language arts teachers and their advisors throughout the year to manage their portfolios. Language arts teachers helped students with the technical aspects of putting together a professional-looking project. Advisors helped students physically manage their portfolios by making sure the students put the appropriate various pieces of work into them. The portfolios were kept in the advisors' rooms. All teachers are advisors, so they helped all of the students with their subject part of the project, and each teacher worked with his or her advisory group to maintain the portfolios. The teachers and students worked together to turn the separate pieces of work into a consolidated project. Here's what it looked like:

First, the math teacher put the students into their construction companies, and they worked on the itemized bids. Later, the language arts teacher had the students add a cover letter, format their bids, and put it all in a presentation folder. In science class, the students considered possible environmental issues as they determined the costs for building the decks. A little later the students studied the local history, and the social studies teacher had the students write a fictitious history of their construction company based on the real history of the area. Along the way, the students crafted numerous revisions, with the appropriate teachers giving the students extra credit and signing off on the project again.

Students documented mastery of skills when they added examples of their work to their portfolios. The portfolio elements were not just random examples of work, but rather a combination that became an impressive project. The language arts teacher was able to reference the different styles of writing the students used when working on the various parts of the project to document mastery of several writing standards. For example, when students worked on the revisions of the history of their construction companies, they were polishing their narrative writing skills.

The elective teachers are integral in establishing learning connections. In fact, as most interdisciplinary projects develop, the elective teachers play the central roles.

It has been my experience that as this process goes forward, many of the projects actually originate in the elective classes. So it is critical that the elective teachers work on the curriculum maps weekly, as they will find the students are applying many of the core skills in their classes.

In the deck project, the language arts teacher and math teacher work with the technology teacher to teach the students about spreadsheets and publishing. As the students cycle through the exploratory classes, the industrial tech teacher helps the students build scale models of their decks for display, the business teacher works with the students on marketing, and the media specialist helps the students put together multimedia bid presentations. The students add to their project at different times in different exploratory classes throughout the year. *(Notice the important collaboration between the core and the exploratory teachers.)*

Near the end of the school year, the student construction companies produce bid presentations for school board and community members. By the time students make their bid presentations, they have an impressive product to share. Each student will have published a binder with the cover letter, a bid created on spreadsheets, their company's environmental policy, and a history of their company. They will have scale models of the decks and, as a company, will make a multimedia bid presentation.

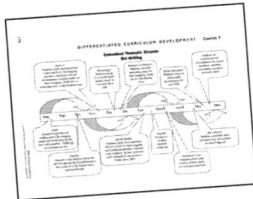

I have included on page 176 a graphic demonstrating the organization of this project. Note how the skills and topics spiral and thread through the school year.

There is a blank form on page 177 for departments to use to show where skills are currently taught and where they might be expanded.

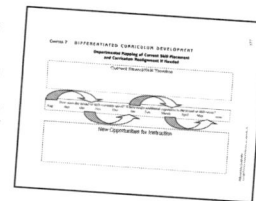

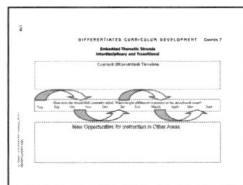

On page 178 is a blank form for any team to use to develop interdisciplinary skills use across the content areas.

On page 179 are examples of how teachers have used this form.

On pages 173 and 174 are two different planning charts. Reproduce one of these or create one of your own to plan for interdisciplinary curriculum projects.

Examples of the ways actual academic teams used the charts are included on pages 172 and 175.

More Advantages for Interdisciplinary Project-Based Learning

What happens to the student who moves in sometime during the year and comes into the project somewhere in the middle? Students moving in and out of schools during the year have always been an issue, and in some areas a very large issue. This is another reason for yearlong projects. These projects make it easier to bring new students up to speed when they move into a class.

When a student moves in, he or she is given copies of the work completed thus far for the project. The project puts the classwork into the context of the team project. The new student adds new work to the project along with other students. One bonus is that the new student becomes part of a "construction company" and has several students to collaborate with from the very first day in class.

Remember that all of the core teachers and many of the exploratory teachers are using the yearlong project. Since the project is interdisciplinary and therefore crosses several curriculum areas, the new student has a common thread to help him or her get to know all of the teachers. That means the student can ask for help on this one project in the technology class, the math class, the English class, the art class, the science class, and . . . *(You get the idea!)*.

*M*any teachers and teams I work with are in highly transient areas such as locations where migrant families live and work. As these teachers work with the COWs and develop cross-curriculum, ongoing projects, they report the learning connections and interdisciplinary projects help them bring new students up to speed. Some students will leave school at some time during the year, and come back again as their parents move for work. It is nice for these students to be a part of the project before they leave, and then get their own portfolios back again when they return.

Shared Assessment Items

Administrative teams have to be concerned with student performance on the state assessments. Leaders will want to demonstrate how the assessment process can be improved through this process as well. As an interdisciplinary project develops during the year, each teacher passes on the assessment they have used. The subsequent teachers will use assessment items from previous assessments, as is appropriate, in their classes. Sometimes, the assessment items need a little tweaking, but most often they can be used verbatim. It is easy to tag those assessment items to demonstrate to the students when and where they had previously had that very same assessment item.

As teachers find and develop other learning connections, the students will participate in many projects during the school year. Each of the projects is started by finding learning connections where skills from one area can be used in another area. All projects are developed from combinations of learning connections, and each project is always built upon required skills.

Since the state test items for the skills are attached to the curriculum maps, the teachers will use those questions as a part of the instruction and assessment that is being developed and shared between content areas. So, some of the shared assessment items are also state test items. Just imagine the items showing up multiple times in multiple content areas, and yet always in context. Remember, this includes the related arts classes as well. (And just when you thought that it could not possibly get any better, we begin to develop common assessments!)

The administrative team should keep in mind that on occasion these learning connections happen in such a way that they become an interdisciplinary teaching unit (IDU). The only difference between the deck project described and a traditional IDU is the timing. The learning connections in the deck project did not happen simultaneously. In an IDU, learning connections are done simultaneously in a given time period. Let the natural timing of the learning connections determine how they are designed (more about IDUs later).

Coordinating Curriculum with Special Programs such as "Magnet Programs," etc.

The COWs are also incredibly helpful in threading magnet strands through core classes. A school may have three magnet programs like business, engineering, and health/medical. Students' exploratory classes for the most part will be in those fields. Sometimes teams are set up according to the academies, but it is much more likely that teachers teach math, English, history, or science and have students from two or even all three programs on their team and in the same class at the same time. So, the question becomes how to design classes with connections to all of these magnet programs. If one teacher had to independently plan a variety of experiences targeted toward the different strands, it would be a huge task, and very time consuming.

The COWs provide a quick reference guide for core teachers to reference examples of topics and activities from different elective/related arts/exploratory programs that are easily incorporated into their classes, and vice versa. Teachers can ask the exploratory teachers to share assignments, activities, and assessments that relate to their core subject. The core teachers can then begin to create assignments and activities relevant to what different students will experience in their specific programs. The core teachers share the state standards and corresponding assessment items which, in turn, become part of the elective/related arts/exploratory assessments.

Most magnet programs are driven by the exploratory classes, so the exploratory teachers should be working with the COWs every week, looking at the core subjects and offering suggestions to the core teachers. This way, the core teachers are able to offer "guided choice" assignments based on the magnet strands and the suggestions of the magnet teachers.

The language arts teacher may give students a choice of three different topics for their narrative paragraphs based on experiences that have already happened in the three magnet strands. This helps maintain the integrity and identity of the various academies within a single class.

The exploratory teachers have the examples and activities, so by using the COWs teachers save planning time. Of course, the core classes are built around the state standards for each area, which means as students participate in interdisciplinary projects, they will be addressing the state standards and assessment examples in the exploratory and magnet classes. In this way, the state standards are cross-referenced between the exploratory and core subjects, as well as among the core subjects. *(This means your school will continually improve student performance on those pesky state tests!)*

Differentiate Instruction Naturally

With each learning connection, teachers naturally differentiate their instruction. Different subjects naturally appeal to different learning styles and intelligences. By bringing other subjects into a class, teachers appeal to different learning styles and intelligences. Consider the following chart which shows some of the learning connections one math teacher found.

```
┌─────────────────────────────────────────────────────┐
│  Differentiating Math Through Learning Connections  │
│      Subject Areas              Topics              │
│   ■ Math—Art              Line Design               │
│   ■ Math—Science          Graph Data                │
│   ■ Math—Life Skills      Exponents                 │
│   ■ Math—Social Studies   Projections               │
│   ■ Math—P.E.             Personal Graphs           │
│   ■ Math—Language Arts    Write Expressions         │
│   ■ Math—Technology       Spreadsheets              │
│   ■ Math—Music            Fractions                 │
│   ■ Math—Business         Percents                  │
│   ■ Math—Shop             Scale Models              │
│   ■ Math—Vocal Music      Raps/Songs for Formulas   │
└─────────────────────────────────────────────────────┘
```

This list is only a beginning. With each learning connection, another teacher in the building helps the math teacher with examples and activities. As a result, other teachers have thus helped the math teacher incorporate the multiple intelligences and all the learning modalities.

I have developed several forms to help teachers plan and document learning connections. Teachers record which subjects are involved in the learning connection and the expected timelines. Then the teachers indicate shared activities. They also document the multiple intelligences addressed by each teacher in the learning connection. There is a vertical learning connection planning chart on page 173 and examples of completed charts on page 172. There is a horizontal learning connection planning chart on page 174 and completed examples on page 175.

As teachers struggle to differentiate instruction and meet the needs of the widely diverse student populations, it is important that administrative teams find easy ways for them to share strategies. Teachers have always shared and developed instructional strategies within their various departments. The teachers in each department have worked to ensure that the state standards are being met and students receive quality instruction. It is imperative that teachers share strategies, activities, and assessments across departmental lines. Cross-referencing strategies, activities, and assessments between departments is the only way to further improve on the quality departmental work that has been done. Using an integrated approach to develop curriculum guarantees that differentiated instruction is going to happen naturally. It also guarantees that the learning experience becomes more relevant for the student. Finally, the state standards are automatically cross-referenced and repeated in multiple subject areas. That means students will perform better on the high-stakes state assessments.

"Old School" Interdisciplinary Teaching Units

It is a popular misconception that integrating curriculum means that all of the teachers on the team should be involved with the same topic at the same time. This is often referred to as the Interdisciplinary Teaching Unit (IDU), or Thematic Teaching Unit. Getting two teachers to line up their curriculums occasionally is difficult enough. It takes a tremendous amount of collaboration and practice *(not to mention the perfect alignment of the planets)* to pull off an effective interdisciplinary unit.

Most often, the teachers pick a central theme, then work to try to fit their curriculums into the theme. While doing this they often work in isolation. For example, the teachers work together to decide what theme might best fit their subjects, what the time frame will be, and hopefully, what sort of closing activity they might plan. After that, the teachers often work on their own *(quite hard, I might add)* to develop lessons for each subject area that will relate to the theme.

The teachers often fill out some sort of form to indicate what they will be doing in each subject area related to the theme. They usually indicate what GLEs (Grade Level Expectations) will be met during the unit. So let's say that the team decides to develop an "Egyptian" thematic unit. The math teacher will work to redesign lessons or create new lessons to relate the math skills to the Egyptian theme. The science, social studies, language arts, and some related arts teachers will all redesign or create new lessons for the Egyptian unit.

It has been my experience that art teachers receive the most requests to do things for core areas that do relate to what the art curriculum says the art teachers should be doing at any one time.

Since the theme is used in all of the classes for the length of the IDU, students will see how each class can be related to the central theme, but not necessarily to other classes and disciplines. This is particularly evident in classes where the natural flow has been changed to relate to the theme. There are some great math lessons that relate to the pyramids, but the math teacher may not have been ready to teach those math concepts. Sometimes this situation feels forced, and teachers say things like "I had to stop teaching my regular curriculum to participate in the IDU."

Before starting an IDU, every teacher has to ask the same questions.
- What skills might be used in the study of Egypt?
- Are those skills taught in this course?
- Do the skills correspond to state standards to be taught?

- Are the skills new or a review of previously learned skills?
- Do the skills fit into the flow of the class, or will I have to stop my teaching plan to fit into the Egyptian unit?

Teachers work very hard to relate each of their subjects to the theme, but not always to each other's subjects. Instead of taking advantage of the planning process, the teachers' workload is increased, which often leads to more frustration than productivity. Teachers are much more likely to participate in developing ongoing interdisciplinary learning connections if they never have to change the flow and sequence of their subjects.

Remember, build learning connections one at a time, and projects and units will emerge with the essential questions already answered and most of the work already done. Shared skills should be the driving force in learning connections—not just a theme. Pretty quickly sets of learning connections connect to other sets of learning connections, which means four or more teachers are automatically involved.

As ongoing projects emerge naturally from the learning connections, themes begin to evolve from the projects. Since the learning connections are built on shared skills first, the projects and interdisciplinary units that evolve support skills and the state standards. Instead of picking a theme and trying to match skills to the theme, the skill connections came first, and then projects and themes emerged.

Interdisciplinary instruction is not about connecting classes to some theme. Interdisciplinary instruction is about connecting classes through common skills.

Interdisciplinary Units Should Happen Naturally

As I mentioned earlier, timing is everything, and that certainly is true for interdisciplinary teaching "thematic" units (IDUs). Sometimes the sequencing of content areas allows for some flexibility. In science, they may have a series of workbooks that are shared between the science teachers, and they may have to do the workbooks in different orders. The language arts teachers may have the same situation with trade books or novels in their curriculums. The social studies teacher may have to cover the local history sometime during the year, but not at any particular time, and so on.

In these and many more instances, the curriculums allow for varying degrees of flexibility. As administrators know, some curriculums like math are perceived to be much more sequential and inflexible than others. The teachers in each department have developed the most effective sequence for each subject area, which is why we should never force any teacher to change the sequencing of his or her subject.

The nice thing for leaders to point out is that the number of potential learning connections is virtually endless. *(Even the planets come into alignment once in a while.)* As teachers practice developing learning connections, they begin to how see how their subject might better fit with some of the others. Naturally, some of these learning connections will actually happen concurrently between the subjects. That means that occasionally the teachers will find that multiple learning connections may come together nearly simultaneously, and they will have everyone working on a learning project at the same time. Curriculum leaders will want to coach teachers to recognize when a learning project can become a "thematic unit," or IDU. *(Simply give it a name such as "the rainforest unit" or "the national parks unit." Everything else has already been done.)*

Documenting the Learning Connections

Teachers need to document learning connections as they develop them. Use the forms on pages 173 and 174 or develop similar ones. This record is especially helpful for new teachers coming into the team. By looking at learning connections the previous teachers developed, the new teacher has a point of reference, and the "connecting" teachers are automatically invested in the new teacher. The new teacher and current teachers have a foundation on which to build.

These forms are easily duplicated. Feel free to choose any of the forms "as is," or change them and adapt them to your specific needs. Attach any assessments and activities that will be shared.

Conclusion

There are several reasons that this curriculum mapping and sharing process works. The first is that the process is kept very simple and fits the planning that has already taken place within the departments. The teachers never have to change the order of their curriculums or try to force their subject to connect with another subject. All of the connections are created from the natural placement of standards and skills within each of the subject areas.

The process appeals to all three of the learning modalities. The process is very visual. The maps are very colorful with each subject having a color, and the connections being indicated with the various colors of tabs, circles, dots, and so on. The process is also verbal, as the teachers have to talk to each other to discuss the learning connections and write adaptations of shared activities for their classes. The process is also very kinesthetic as the teachers are physically manipulating the various notes, test items, and other things that are attached to curriculum maps. A teacher can walk from one end of a curriculum map to the other and experience week-to-week views of the classes on the map.

Finally, the curriculum mapping procedure presented here has the Involvement Model of Change built into the process. Remember that in this model, the stages are not only incremental (with each stage building on the previous stage), but are also cumulative and constantly repeated throughout the process of change. That means that at the implementation stage, the three previous stages must still be active. So, interest must be continually generated, information must be gathered and shared, and input has to be solicited for the decisions that continue to be made.

In the COW curriculum mapping process, the interest is built in as the teachers only look for learning connections that will benefit their own classes. The process is based on the interest that teachers have for their own subjects and the students they teach. When learning connections are found, the teachers share information about their subject to inform each other about how certain skills are being used in their particular content area. Then the teachers get input about how that information might be used, and make their decisions about how to develop the learning connections. Once the implementation of the COW curriculum mapping process has taken place, there is a continual cycling of interest, information, and input that keeps the process fresh and motivating. This means that the process moves very smoothly into the integration phase of becoming common practice in the school.

TAG . . . You're It!

Getting the Cattle Drive Started

Exercise One

Of course, the first exercise will be for the administrative team to lead the teachers in building the COWs. In one-day workshops, I often have the participants build what you might call a mini-COW. That is what I am going to recommend for this exercise. Maybe we will call these "calves." What the administrative team will need to do is have core and elective teachers get together for this exercise. This is a great activity for a differentiated staff meeting! (See the differentiated staff meetings section).

The curriculum leaders will want to do a presentation about the COWs first. *(If administrative teams or curriculum leaders will contact me, I am happy to send you my Power Point which I use when I present COWs.)* Then have each of the teachers fill in just six of the weekly adhesive notes to randomly represent six topics they each teach during the school year, and put them on piece of poster board. Remember to have a board for the core classes and a separate board for the exploratory classes at each grade level. If your school has teams, then of course, it will be beneficial for the core teachers to work with their team.

Then the leaders will want the teachers to look for learning connections. The leaders will want to give the teachers about 20 minutes to look at the maps. Again, remember to have the core and exploratory teachers look at each other's "calves." Every time I do this exercise, the teachers will find several learning connections. For the next few minutes of the staff meeting, have the teachers each pick one learning connection to discuss and develop. Finally, for the last few minutes of the staff meeting, have some of the teachers share the learning connection they developed. Remember to call on both core and exploratory teachers for the sharing.

Exercise Two

The curriculum leaders will want to work with the departments for this exercise. Leaders will use the COWs, the form on page 173, and state test data disaggregated by skill. First, identify a skill set the department needs to work on and determine when it is currently taught. Then look for opportunities to provide additional exposures within the departments' classes.

Exercise Three

If your school has teams, the administrative team will work with the teams and use the COWs to identify where the skill sets identified by the departments might be used in other curriculum areas. The idea here is to find learning connections based on the skills selected by the departments in the previous exercise. The form on page 177 may be useful in identifying the timeline for spiraling and threading the learning connections. Then look for opportunities to create ongoing projects and/or interdisciplinary units.

Differentiated Leadership
Copyright ©2008 by Incentive Publications, Inc., Nashville, TN.

Integrated Curriculum Learning Connections Planning Chart

For Correlating Topics, Timelines, Shared Assessments, Focus Activities,
Project Development, and Differentiated Instruction.

Connecting Areas, Weeks, Timelines, and Topics
Student Performances: Focus Activities, Reference Points, Shared Assignments, Assessments, and More
Standards Achieved: What Questions Will Be Answered? Attach Assessments.
Differentiated Instruction: Shared Strategies, Multiple Intelligences, Learning Styles, and Modalities

Learning Connections Planning Chart

For Correlating Shared Assessments, Focus Activities, Multiple Intelligences, and Differentiated Instruction

CONNECTING AREAS/WKS	CONNECTING TOPICS	SHARED ACTIVITIES, WORKSHEETS, REFERENCE POINTS, ASSESSMENTS, ETC.	LEARNING STYLES (INTELLIGENCES and MODALITIES)

Differentiated Leadership

Learning Connections Planning Chart (SAMPLE)

For Correlating Shared Assessments, Focus Activities, Multiple Intelligences, and Differentiated Instruction

CONNECTING AREAS/WKS	CONNECTING TOPICS	SHARED ACTIVITIES, WORKSHEETS, REFERENCE POINTS, ASSESSMENTS, ETC.	LEARNING STYLES (INTELLIGENCES and MODALITIES)
Math: WK 8–9 SS: WK 28–30	Charts and Graphs with Demographics and Elections.	Some of the math charts and graph worksheets will use information from the demographics already studied in social studies, and with election information to be covered later in SS. Shared state test items will be used in both areas in unit tests.	Verbal/Linguistic—predictions Interpersonal—SS community groups Logical/Mathematical Visual/Spatial—graph, illustrate Body/Kinesthetic—presentations
Math: WK 4 ART: WK 5 of rotation	Line Design with String Art Sculptures	Students will use line designs in math for the base of their string art sculptures. 25% of the math grade will be art sculpture, and 25% of the art grade will be the math designs. Art will use math state test items for angles and measurement in class activities.	Body/Kinesthetic—building sculptures Logical/Mathematical Naturalist—patterns and natural design Intrapersonal—demonstrate, create, etc.
Math—WK 15–16 LA: WK 15	Simplifying Expressions and Writing Sentences	Students will write a cover letter, create spreadsheets, and build a portfolio for their bid projects. The language arts-math grades will be interdependent. They will share and embed state test items in their activities and tests.	Verbal/Linguistic Logical/Mathematical Visual/Spatial—design a cover, etc. Interpersonal—const. companies Naturalist—outdoor projects, envir.
Math—Music Ongoing	Equations and Formulas with Writing Music.	Students will put equations and formulas to music. The music might be a popular song or an original song created by the student. The students will work on the songs in music, and will have to teach the other students the song in math class.	Musical/Rhythmic—setting to music Verbal/Linguistic—composing Logical/Mathematical Visual/Spatial—illustrating, etc. Body/Kinesthetic—dances Interpersonal—performances

Embedded Thematic Strands
Bid Writing

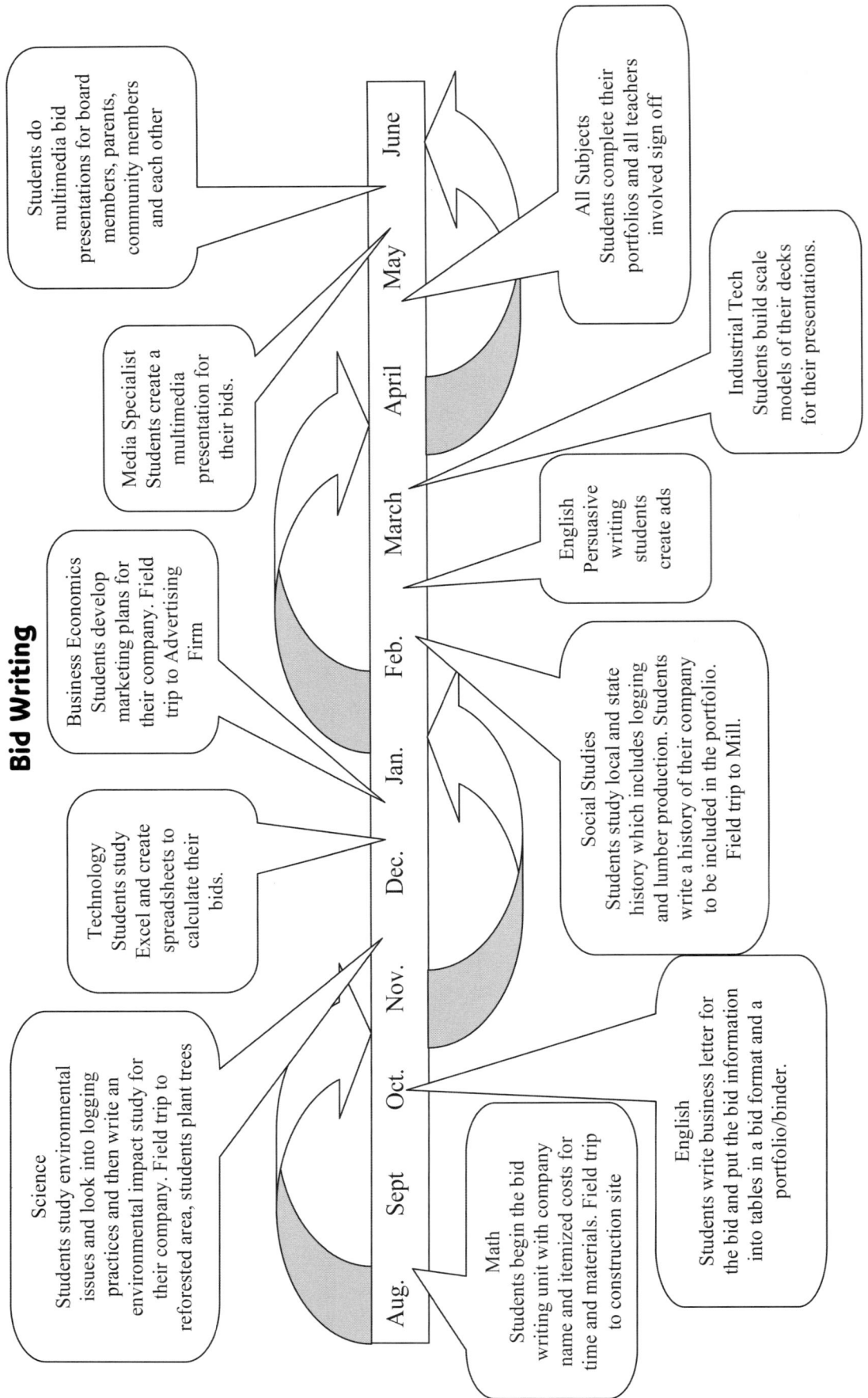

Timeline: Aug. | Sept | Oct. | Nov. | Dec. | Jan. | Feb. | March | April | May | June

Students do multimedia bid presentations for board members, parents, community members and each other

Media Specialist Students create a multimedia presentation for their bids.

Business Economics Students develop marketing plans for their company. Field trip to Advertising Firm

Technology Students study Excel and create spreadsheets to calculate their bids.

Science Students study environmental issues and look into logging practices and then write an environmental impact study for their company. Field trip to reforested area, students plant trees

Math Students begin the bid writing unit with company name and itemized costs for time and materials. Field trip to construction site

English Students write business letter for the bid and put the bid information into tables in a bid format and a portfolio/binder.

Social Studies Students study local and state history which includes logging and lumber production. Students write a history of their company to be included in the portfolio. Field trip to Mill.

English Persuasive writing students create ads

Industrial Tech Students build scale models of their decks for their presentations.

All Subjects Students complete their portfolios and all teachers involved sign off

Differentiated Leadership
Copyright ©2008 by Incentive Publications, Inc., Nashville, TN.

**Departmental Mapping of Current Skill Placement
and Curriculum Realignment if Needed**

Current Strand/Skill Timeline

Aug	Sep	Oct	Nov	Dec	Jan	Feb	March	April	May	June

How does the strand or skill currently spiral? Where might additional exposures to the strand or skill occur?

New Opportunities for Instruction

Embedded Thematic Strands
Interdisciplinary and Transitional

Current Strand/Skill Timeline

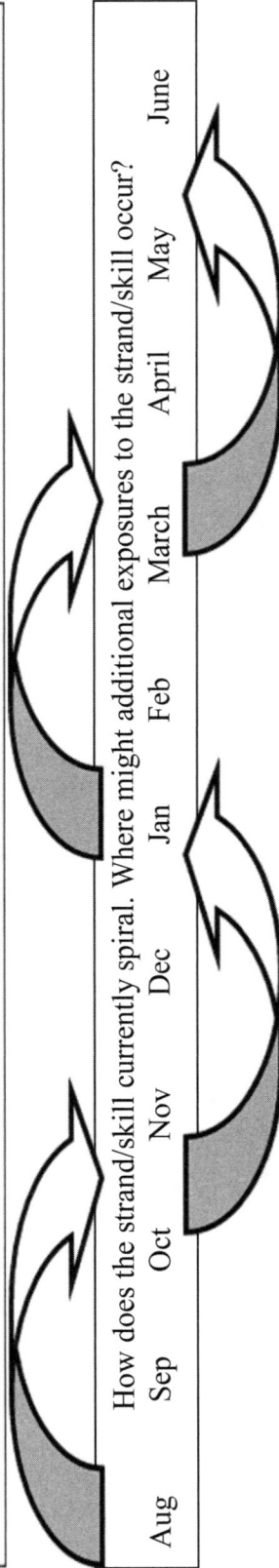

How does the strand/skill currently spiral. Where might additional exposures to the strand/skill occur?

| Aug | Sep | Oct | Nov | Dec | Jan | Feb | March | April | May | June |

New Opportunities for Instruction in Other Areas

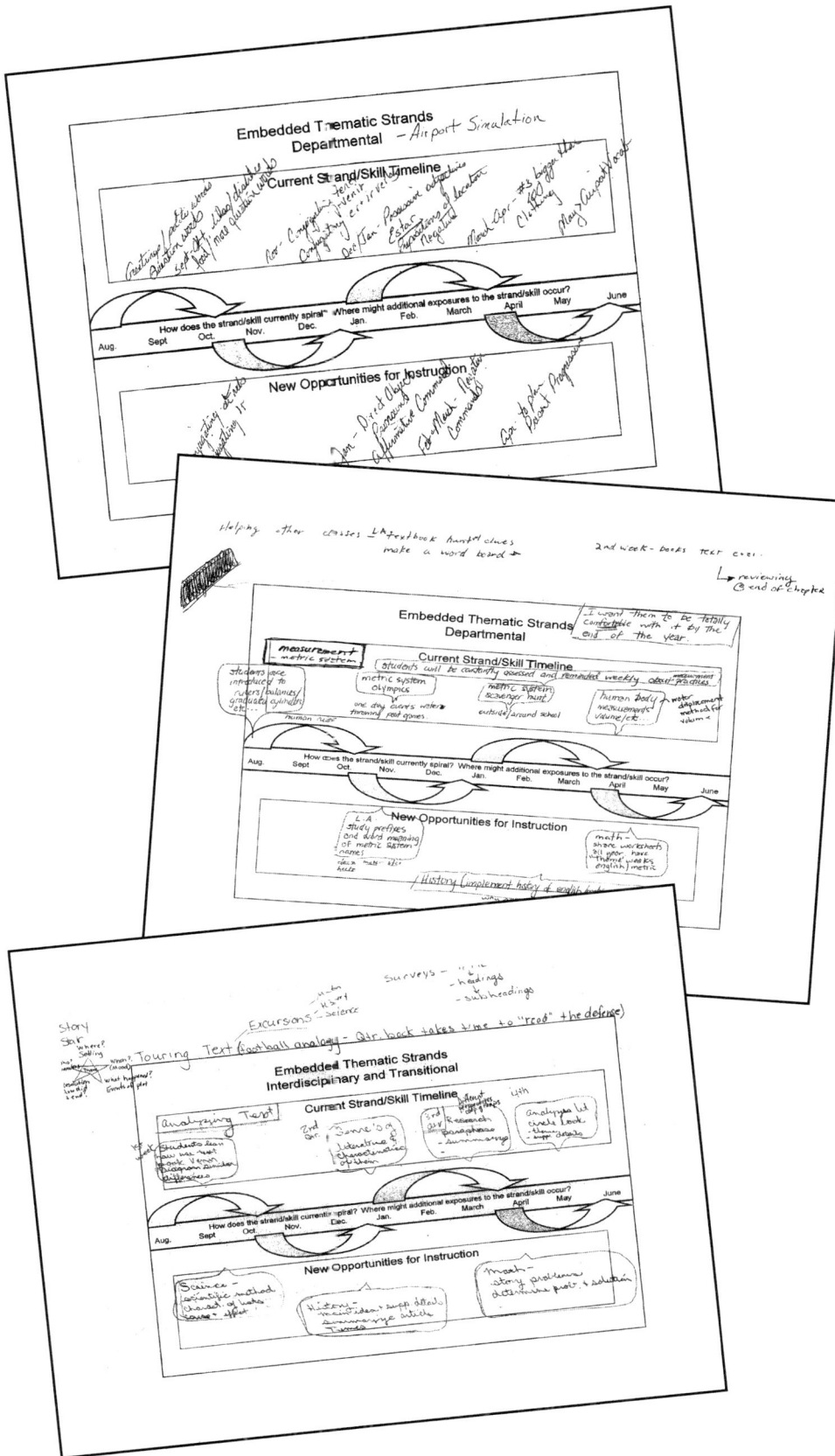

Examples of Spiraling Form

Community & Business Involvement—COMPASS

COMmunity Partnerships Assuring Student Success

Differentiated Leadership Requires Administrators to Think Beyond the Walls of the School Building

Administrators are so intensely involved with issues within their school that developing community involvement beyond parent involvement is almost an afterthought. Most school improvement plans have developing and documenting parent involvement as a part of the program. The bulk of the parent involvement revolves around parent conferences, parent volunteers, and parent-teacher organizations. Most community involvement is restricted to the traditional partnerships that businesses have had with the school. In most schools, even traditional business partnerships can be counted on one hand.

Remember that one of the School Performance Management Systems (SPMS) is parent and community involvement, and that all of the systems are interdependent. So, if we are able to develop meaningful business partnerships, they should also have a positive impact on all of the other systems. The program outlined here gives administrators a way to develop community and business partnerships that will have a positive impact on all of the SPMS. The program I will demonstrate in this chapter is called "COMPASS."

(Administrators know the importance of a good acronym), and COMPASS is one of the best acronyms I have come up with. *COMPASS* stands for *COMmunity Partnerships Assuring Student Success. (This program is the best way I have found to get the business community actively engaged in a meaningful way with the schools.)* COMPASS fits naturally with the systems you have in place. That being said, this program will require that your school have a curriculum mapping system in place.

If your school does not have COWs *(see the previous chapter on curriculum development)* or some similar program, your school will first have to complete that task. COMPASS is a curriculum-based program and requires an easily accessed version of the school's curriculum for the businesses and teachers to use collaboratively. The preceding chapter on curriculum development will lead you through the process of implementing the easiest to build and use interactive curriculum maps.

The next thing you, as administrators, are going to appreciate is the multitude of positive ways this easily initiated program will impact your school. The benefits to the school are almost too many to list, but I will try.

Businesses will see that COMPASS is as beneficial to them as it is to the schools. Creating a symbiotic relationship between the school and the business community is another demonstration of differentiated leadership.

Show Me the Benefits!
How COMPASS Can Help Your School Program

Teachers often ask administrators why a change needs to occur and how it will help students. Developing the COMPASS program is good for the school and students, so teachers will do whatever it takes to make it happen regardless of the effort. COMPASS will be one of the easier programs you will have to sell to your staff. The ultimate selling point is just how easy the program is to implement.

★ The benefits will
sell the program.

★ The simplicity of the
program gets it going.

★ The symbiotic nature of
the program will sustain
it once under way.

Administrators and teachers will appreciate the authentic ways the school becomes linked to the community. As a part of the program, the business partners work with the teachers to share examples of how skills identified in the curriculum maps are actually applied in real-world business settings. By using the business examples in their classrooms, the teachers' lessons become real and relevant for their students. All teachers have to handle situations where students are asking "When am I ever going to use this?" The teachers need to have answers to use that are realistic. The business can give the teachers answers from real-world applications. That makes the learning relevant for students.

Another point becomes clear to teachers and administrators as their schools work with more businesses. It is inevitable that some of the employees of the various businesses are also parents of students at the school. Since most all of the parents from a school also work in the area, it only makes sense that the more business relationships schools develop, the more parents will get involved via the business connection. This means that another byproduct of COMPASS is that more families are actively engaged with the school. This benefit really expands when you recognize how many extended family members are also working in the various businesses, and will now be working with the schools as a result of COMPASS.

Every year budgets get tighter, and administrators have to do more with fewer and fewer resources. Another benefit of COMPASS is that the business will often provide materials to make the lessons more real and relevant. A few simple examples would include businesses giving teachers things like: business letterhead for students to write business letters, actual inventory sheets, bid sheets, amortization worksheets, savings account tally sheets, payment worksheets for a car or house loan, spreadsheets of all kinds, travel brochures, and many more.

The good news for the students, teachers, and businesses is that the students are taking home worksheets provided by the businesses. These are real-world tools and not teacher-made examples. This makes the work authentic for the students. Of course, you have probably already guessed that this is also great advertising for the participating businesses. That means that the students, teachers, administrators, and businesses involved all benefit from the opportunity of having 150 students each taking home worksheets with the name of local businesses on them.

As the program grows, more people from the businesses will come to the school to work with the teachers in a variety of ways. Administrators will want to encourage the business partners to do presentations, bring materials, and supplement

instruction in a variety of ways for the topics they have chosen. *(As an administrator, one of the more real advantages for me turned out to be the benefits of having more adults in the building. Most often, these are adults that the students know and recognize as providing help to the instructional program from the businesses, as well as being some student's parent, uncle, aunt or a student's friend's parent, uncle or aunt, or so on. As the program grew, in my personal experience, having extra adults in the classrooms, in the hallways, and in the cafeteria was a huge bonus.)* Administrators and teachers will quickly realize that COMPASS generates both supplemental materials and human resources in support of the instructional program.

COMPASS Benefits Schools

★ Makes curriculum real and relevant

   Businesses provide actual examples of the application of skills taught in the curriculum.

★ Connects school with the community

   The program creates a symbiotic relationship between the school and the businesses in the program.

★ Reengages families in the education of students

   Many family members work in the businesses that participate in the program.

★ Supplements school resources—human, materials, field trips

   The school uses hard-copy examples from the business. Business people come to the school to help teachers deliver the curriculum.

★ Updates the school on current trends in business

   The school and the curriculum are constantly being updated with current business practices.

★ Helps the business community understand the educational system and its challenges

   The business community gets a firsthand look at the resources the school has, as well as the challenges and demands the school faces.

Given today's fast-paced changes, it can be difficult for schools to remain current with the real-world applications of the skills they are teaching. We all know just how quickly technology changes, and since everything is influenced by technology, it is critical that administrators and teachers find ways to keep up with the most current applications. Only by working with businesses can schools hope to stay up-to-date with current business trends and skill applications. This is certainly just the tip of the iceberg, but the idea is that the business partners become integral components of the schools' curriculum, and then the schools will stay on top of the most current applications of the skills teachers are trying to teach.

Finally, COMPASS also develops a great amount of empathy for the schools by the businesses. I have personally heard innumerable times people from the business community make remarks about what a great job the teachers do in the face of the challenges they face. I think sometimes we in education worry about having people from the community in our buildings. However, when they become an integral part of the program, and they are helping the teachers from the skill and curriculum development level, I have found that these business people become all the more appreciative of the school's efforts. Differentiated leadership is also about getting the community invested in the school's progress and success.

Getting Your Bearings with this COMPASS

The first thing for administrators to realize is that COMPASS is a curriculum-based program. The partnerships that are going to be established are going to be created around topics and skills that relate to both the business and what is being taught in the various curriculums. That means that there has to be a tool to enable the communications between the business community and the teachers. The curriculum guides for each subject are far too detailed and voluminous for any person at a business to review even one curriculum guide, much less look over all of the curriculums.

This is why curriculum mapping comes into play, and especially the COWs. They are visual representations of the curriculums with an outline of every course in the school. As you know from the previous chapter, the outlines are general in description, showing only the main content that is being taught each week of each course. Since the information included on the maps is generic, it is very easy for anyone, including business people, to review the major topics that are being taught in several courses of study in a short period of time. This appeals to people in business because for them, time really is money. *(I find that one of the reasons this process works for the business community is the fact that it is not time- or labor-intensive, so it will be a minimal distraction for the businesses.)*

With that in mind, it is critical that the COWs (curriculum maps) explained in the previous chapter on curriculum development not only be in place, but that they have been in use for a period of time prior to implementing the COMPASS program. In the book *Get Fit!* I recommend that teachers use the maps for a year before attempting the COMPASS program. *(It may not take a full year. You will have to gauge the readiness of the staff before starting the program. Remember once again the Involvement Model of Change and be sure to get the input of the staff about their comfort level with using the COWs before adding COMPASS to their plate.)*

Teachers and administrators need to be very comfortable with the COWs, and need to have developed several "learning connections" before attempting to get the community involved. When the maps have been in place for a while, and the teachers have had the opportunity to practice developing learning connections, they will have had a chance to refine the process. With practice, the teachers will plan efficiently. The practice with developing learning connections builds confidence, and the teachers and administrators will have many examples of learning connections to share with the business people. When the administrative team and the teachers are ready, they will be able to make better presentations to the business community.

FOUR POINTS OF COMPASS

1. Build the curriculum maps (COWs).
2. Find learning connections and realign curriculums as needed.
3. Discuss and develop the learning connections between the content areas.
4. Share the COWs with businesses, so they can identify learning connections between the curriculums and their businesses.
   a. Businesses look for topics and skills that are part of the curriculum and that are necessary for success in their businesses as well.
   b. Teachers meet with business members to discuss what form the learning connections will take in the classroom.

Making the Businesses Part of the Herd

When the administrative team is confident that the teachers are ready to get the business community involved, the first task for the administrative team will be to contact several businesses about the possibility of becoming part of the program.

One school that I work with had a staff meeting to brainstorm ways that someone on the staff could make personal contact with businesses. That way, there was at least a very good chance of getting in the door to speak with someone at the business. I have found that if I can just get to talk to someone of the appropriate authority in a business, that business will usually become a part of the program. As you will see, the program practically sells itself when it is presented.

Another great way to get business leads is to present COMPASS at a parent meeting. Most of your parents will work somewhere in the community. Therefore, they can suggest businesses that might be interested in the program, as well as exactly with whom to make the initial contact. In some instances, the parents might go back to the business where they work and share enough of the program to get the ball rolling.

A third approach which enables representatives of your school to access many businesses at once is for the administrative team and teachers to make a presentation at a chamber of commerce meeting. Let them know that the presentation will be brief and that you will need only about 15 minutes of the meeting time to present what's happening at your school. Get the appropriate contact information to be able to follow up with any businesses that express an interest at the meeting. Then, someone from the school should visit with each of the businesses. Visiting a business is more labor-intensive and time-consuming initially, but it is incredibly effective.

Finally, another school I know sent invitations out to businesses the staff had listed for a business open house at their school.

**Note to administrators: This can work really well
if you have staff members deliver the invitations**

and personally invite the businesses to your open house. *(If you have any sort of parent and business evening meetings, of course, have good food available at the meeting. That is the old "feed them and they will come" philosophy, which continues to work well.)*

Leaders need to keep all initial meetings and presentations short and to the point. Remind businesses that all of the follow-up meetings as a part of the program will also be very short. As I said earlier, this is another bonus since it suits the business community. They are not going to have to give extended periods of time to the school, which would mean extended periods of time away from the business. I have found that most of the meetings will generally be less than 30 minutes, so the presentations should also be short.

Now that you are in front of the businesses, whether it is at an evening meeting, a chamber of commerce meeting, or at the business location, I want to walk the administrative team through the presentation. It will always be better if a few teachers can be a part of the presentation as well. The team making the presentation will have to have one or more of the curriculum maps to use for the presentation. If the meeting is actually at the business, it is effective to leave the curriculum map at the business should the business choose to participate. If this is going to be an evening event at the school, then have the meeting where all of the curriculum maps can be put up for display.

Hopefully, the administrative team has documented the original curriculum mapping workshops with digital pictures. If your school has pictures of the development and implementation of the COW process, then you might also want to begin all COMPASS appearances with a short PowerPoint presentation. The presentation team will want to share what the COWs are, and give several examples of learning connections that teachers have already developed or are currently working on. It would be nice if the learning connections were presented by the teachers involved in developing them.

The presentation team will need to have the COW materials that the business will be using. These would include a few adhesive notes, dots, stars, tabs of various colors for the business to add their input. (See the previous chapter for a more detailed description of the materials needed). Someone from the presentation team will need to demonstrate how the information is arranged on the adhesive notes. Show the businesses that the number in the upper corner indicates the number of the week that the content is being taught; the content that is being taught is written in the middle of the adhesive note in very generic terms; and the numbers and letters on the bottom of the adhesive note represent any state standards that are included with the content for that week. This would be a good time to show how the teachers have also attached sample state test questions on the map.

Now the presentation team will want to demonstrate what a learning connection is. Be careful to demonstrate specific examples of how teachers share assignments, assessments, activities, etc., between two different areas. Share examples of how students can get multiple grades in multiple areas for doing one assignment, and so on. Your school may not have developed ongoing projects as yet, but be sure to share how several learning connections can turn into interdisciplinary projects.

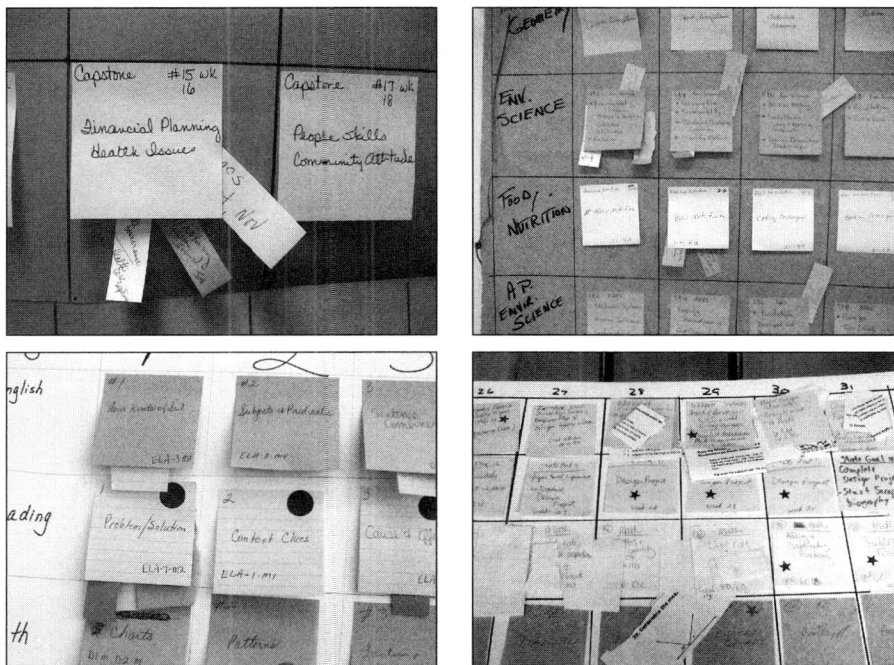

Share sample maps with the businesses to demonstrate learning connections, how the dots are used, and how the sample state assessment items are correlated with the curriculums.

The presentation group will want to make sure that the business people understand what all of the dots, tabs, etc., actually mean on the maps. Demonstrate how the various shapes and colors on the maps allow teachers and administrators to track things like the use of technology, the media center, and writing across the curriculum, among other things. I want the community to see how the COWs simplify the many intricate and complex curriculums into easy-to-read weekly outlines of the courses, and then the many ways that the curriculum maps can be used.

It's Time to Get the Cattle Drive Started!

The presentation team will now want the businesses to see how they can use the maps. Invite the business people to come up and experience the curriculum maps. Ask them to look over the maps and read the adhesive notes. You want them to see the different topics that are taught in each of the subjects in each of the grade levels. The business people should be looking for any topic or skill that is listed on the maps that they also use in their business. The task for the business people is to look for topics in the curriculums that might require skills which are also skills required as a part of their business. The idea is for the business people to be able to provide a teacher with examples from their business that demonstrate skills found on the curriculum maps.

For example, the business may have examples of math or writing that the teachers could use as real-world examples or even student work. Students can then use a *real* sheet from a *real* business to learn or practice skills. Remember that the examples from the business are ones that relate to topics and skills on the curriculum maps, which as you know, are correlated to the state test standards. Now some of the student homework has a business name on top and is an actual sheet used by the business. So the homework assignment becomes more real and relevant to the students. When a business finds this type of opportunity, it's a learning connection between the teacher and the business.

When the businesses find learning connections, they can work with the teachers in any combination of four ways. First, the business personnel might have stories and verbal examples of how the skills in the learning connections are used in the business settings. That way the teachers can enhance their lessons by sharing real-world examples from the stories that people from the businesses have shared with them. Second, the business people might have hard copy of forms like bid sheets, estimate sheets, form letters, and so on, that could be used in the classroom. Businesses might also have instructional videos that could be used by the teachers. For example, they might have instructional videos for lab safety which could be shown to students to demonstrate how their science labs are really preparing them for possible jobs in real-world lab settings.

The third thing a business can do is to have someone from the business come in person and talk to the students personally about a particular topic or skill. Personal appearances are always powerful ways to demonstrate real-world applications to students. Instead of having the fire department come in and talk generically about being fire fighters, they come in and do presentations on heat transfer, PSI, or flammable compounds in various science classes, and only when the students are actually studying those topics. The students will get a better view of the skills involved in different professions, if the actual professionals come in when the students are studying those particular skills.

Finally, the businesses might provide on-site examples for the students which, of course, we call field trips. Because any field trips will come from the development of learning connections, the field trips will be tied to specific skills that the students are learning about. The field trips are actually field studies as the students are going to observe and learn more about specific skills in practice.

With the development of learning connections, field trips take on new significance for both the students and the businesses. With this in mind, students from an English class might visit the newspaper several times in a school year instead of one generic visit. One trip to the newspaper might be for some students to look just at the editing process, because they are editing and doing rewrites in their class at the time. Later, some students might visit to look at the distribution process as a part of their business exploratory class. Then students will go back later to look at advertising, as they learn about marketing in the business exploratory class, as well as persuasive writing in the English class.

Notice that the English teacher and the business exploratory teacher will also be collaborating with each other. This will probably be an opportunity for some sort of long-term project. Now field trips are targeted toward specific topics and skills the teacher is trying to develop with the help of the business. In this case, all students will not necessarily go on all field trips. Some students will sign up for the editing process trip, others for advertising, and others still for looking at the reporting processes, and so on, depending on what they are doing in English class and what exploratory class they are in at the time.

WAYS FOR A BUSINESS TO PARTICIPATE

1. Share stories and examples with the teacher to use in the classroom to make the lesson more real and relevant.

2. Share *hard-copy* examples that show one application of the skill in the business. This might include the forms the business uses, pictures, videos, and brochures.

3. Someone from the business visits the class to share stories and examples in person and to demonstrate how a particular skill is used in the business.

4. Provide field experience opportunities. Students visit the business to view and actually experience firsthand how the skill is applied in the business.

Administrative teams and teachers also report that another skill area the students develop as a result of working with people in business is the affective/soft skills/people skill area that is so critical for success on the job. The learning connections will be built on specific cognitive skills identified on the curriculum maps; but in the process of helping students learn those skills, business people will almost certainly also talk about affective skills.

Affective skills include things like working well with other employees, being prepared, being motivated, being empathetic with customers, getting to work on time, not being tardy from lunch or other breaks, having a good attitude, and so much more. Of course, as students begin to develop these skills, they are also going to be much more successful in school. If your school has an advisory program, the business community can be of tremendous assistance to teachers regarding such affective skills as those mentioned here, and which advisory programs are designed to develop.

Finally, another real bonus for schools is the understanding that the business community acquires about the demands placed on educators. This becomes especially true in regard to the resources and materials educators have to get the job done. The more time a business spends in a school, the more the people from the business

Differentiated Leadership
Copyright ©2008 by Incentive Publications, Inc., Nashville, TN.

have the opportunity see the really great things that are going on. In my experience, the business community becomes a real advocate for the school and can help the administrative team dispel rumors and mistruths that sometimes get going in the community. The businesses will help get the good word out about the school.

"If you're the one leading the herd, it is a good thing to look around once in a while to make sure they are still following you!"

—from the book
Don't Squat With Your Spurs On!

What Will the Businesses Get Out of This?

I talked about COMPASS creating a symbiotic relationship between the businesses and the school. That means that there are also benefits for the business that make their efforts worthwhile. The first and most obvious benefit for each business is that COMPASS is a tremendous and *very cost-effective public relations* program for the business. I have had business people share that they were happy to be helping in such a meaningful way, but it did not hurt that this was also the best advertising they had ever done. Of course they often throw in phrases like *cost-effective, efficiency, value added*, and . . . you get the idea.

Administrators need to know that the business community wants to support schools; in fact, community service is often built into their business model. However, leaders have lacked the tools to facilitate the communication between the staff at the school and the employees at the business. Because of that, when partnerships were formed they had to be fairly generic and involve limited communication—usually between a contact person at the school and a contact person at the business. This dramatically reduces the level of involvement that is possible for the business, regardless of their willingness to help.

In fact, any number of employees at a business could possibly help with a wide variety of subjects and topics within the school. For example, business personnel from marketing, sales, distribution, secretarial, management, maintenance, and so on, would see the curriculum maps differently since they all use a variety of skills in the workplace. As a math teacher, I can tell you that the number of possible contacts between the number of employees at a business and the number of staff members at a school will create a humongous amount of workable combinations. *(Humongous: one of those very technical mathematical terms to designate very large numbers.)* The COWs make any number of combinations possible, and actually fairly easy to coordinate.

With the COWs, the businesses have a tool to allow them to look over several content areas quickly and identify how, when, and exactly where they might be of the most assistance. Another bonus for the business is that anyone at the business can have valuable input into the process. *(In one business that I worked with, two of the maintenance employees found some of the best learning connections. These two maintenance employees made some of the best classroom presentations that I have seen.)* The business person that finds the potential learning connection to a topic simply tags it with a star, dot, or tab to let the teacher know. Then, as the teacher begins to prepare for that unit of instruction, he or she will contact the appropriate person at the business. To get even more of the business employees engaged as described here, the administrative team should encourage the initial business contact person to take the COW back to the place of business for a week or two.

The administrative team must be sensitive to the fact that time is a critical resource for both the business community and the school staff. Leaders in both settings realize their staffs have limited amounts of time for planning and want to get the most out of any planning time they can have. Since COMPASS targets the business involvement precisely to a specific topic and teacher, the discussion and development of the business participation is done effectively and efficiently.

The business community is counting on informed consumers, especially in regards to their goods and services. Therefore, another benefit for the businesses is getting information about their business out to current and future consumers. Students develop knowledge about how the skills they are developing are applied in specific business settings. As parents work with their children on worksheets and other materials provided by a business, they are much more likely to understand how that business functions. Not too far down the road, the students are going to become adult consumers as well. So the students will leave school with up-close and personal information about the workings of the businesses in the community.

Another great need for the businesses in any community is the availability of a qualified workforce. The students that are benefiting from applying skills in real business settings will also soon be in the workforce. With COMPASS, the teachers and the business community will know that the students are being taught the specific cognitive skills they are going to need to be successful employees.

As I mentioned earlier, community service is often built into a company's business model. Schools are also involved in community service, and in most instances, they can combine efforts with their business partners to increase the results that would be possible if the two were only working independently. This will be another area that will enhance the business's image in the community, and the school can be of great assistance to the business in their community service efforts.

Linking the community service component above with an ongoing environmental interdisciplinary unit, the students in one school, with the cooperation of several businesses, actually created their own city park. The city donated the land, and the students, assisted by several businesses (like a local lumber company), created a park for endangered species of trees. Imagine all the learning connections that come together in developing and maintaining a city park. The park is there year-round, and so then are the learning connections.

Finally, as an administrator, I experienced one business that had been working with our students extensively for two years, and one of the areas was in the computer lab. The business had generously upgraded our lab to be able to run some of their "CAD" software. That is when the business also realized that they could use our lab to do some of their training of new employees. I scheduled the lab a couple of evenings a week for their use. The business would hold training in the lab, or try out new software, which meant that the business had to keep our lab up-to-date in order to handle their software. *(Not to run the business catch phrases into the ground, but this was truly a win-win situation.)*

There is one more area which I think benefits both the business community and schools. I have found that building a strong COMPASS program means a much greater support from the business community for issues like local bonds or state tax proposals. Having multiple businesses actively engaged in the instructional program at your school dramatically increases the chances that school-based tax proposals will be passed when they are put out there by the school system. Imagine if several businesses were also making calls, putting signs out, and taking ads in the various media—only this time, in support of the bond issue! If the business community is actually in the schools and can experience what is happening from the curriculum up, they will have much greater insight into our goals and needs.

COMPASS Benefits Businesses

★ Great public relations

Business expertise and resources help teachers teach and students learn.

★ Cost-effective way to advertise

Imagine 130 students working with supplies provided by a business.

★ Preparation of future employees

Students will be in the work force at some point.

★ More knowledgeable consumers

Students share with parents what they have learned about the businesses and their products.

★ Better understanding and appreciation in schools of the challenges and needs of business

Students and teachers get an up-close and personal look at businesses.

★ Supplement business resources

The students can develop advertising and do number crunching for the businesses.

Students can create posters and put together print and television ads.

Schools can become off-site learning centers for businesses.

★ Better understanding of the education process

Businesses learn about learning.

Businesses become more "brain-based" after working with the educators to develop curriculum and assessments.

★ Community service

Businesses report their employees increase involvement in community service projects after getting involved with COMPASS.

Remember to Showcase the Program and Celebrate the Success!

(You will not be surprised that my favorite way to get more than two people together in one place is to have great food available!) One of the most successful methods of getting the business community and the school together, along with parents and other interested community members, is to sponsor a community breakfast. *(I am talking about breakfasts that might compete with Cracker Barrel here!)* Initially, the school may sponsor the breakfasts,

but I have found that after something like this is begun, businesses want to sponsor them. When enough businesses are involved, you may have them take turns sponsoring the breakfasts. What your school should do is highlight one or more of the businesses and the specific lessons that have been developed by the business and the teachers.

The administrative team should assist the teachers and businesses involved with the development of the initial presentations. It is important that, when showcasing teaching units developed with the cooperation of the business, you have some of the students, teachers, and business members that were involved be a part of the presentation. I encourage administrators and teachers to take lots of digital pictures of the students and teachers working with the businesses during the lesson. These can then be used for the PowerPoint presentation at the breakfast, and for sending to the local newspaper. Be sure to encourage teachers to put together a few handouts for the breakfasts that were made with some of the student work, as well as the assessments that were used in the unit. It is important that the state-assessed skills be highlighted as a part of the presentation.

I also want to share another way to increase teachers' understanding of how the skills they are teaching are applied in the business setting, and that is a teacher-employee switch. For many obvious reasons, the teacher-employee switch can only be for a very short period of time, but it is valuable if the teacher can spend some time in the business setting. It is also invaluable for the business to understand what it is like to try to get a student to understand a concept. Be careful, however: I know of a school that lost a science teacher one time to a business. The business offered the science teacher a job after the science teacher had spent some time at the business. The school lost a science teacher, but gained an enthusiastic advocate for the school in the business!

The administrative team should make sure that the students send some of their work to the business. The students should share work that demonstrates how they are applying the examples that were supplied by the business. Of course, a plaque or some sort of framed certificate of appreciation could always be presented to participating businesses, at some very public event like the community breakfasts.

Once the business community begins to spend time in the school in meaningful ways, the interaction between the business community and the staff will happen naturally. One more way I found to get the business partners and the school staff together is staff-partner activities. For example, one school sponsors staff-partner ski evenings at a nearby ski resort once a month during ski season. In another school, the teachers have formed bowling and softball teams with the business partners and compete in the local city bowling and softball leagues.

WAYS TO GET EVERYONE TOGETHER
- Community breakfasts
- Feed them and they will come!
- Showcase teaching units
- Teacher-Employee switches
- Field trips to business
- Staff-Partner Activities
- Ski nights
- Join a softball or bowling league with the business partner, and so on

Differentiated Leadership is About Putting the Puzzle Together

I have shared the Involvement Model of Change, the three levels of personal responsibility, and the eight school performance management systems with you in this book. These represent the many complex pieces of the successful school puzzle. COMPASS is a program designed to help schools pull many of the pieces of that puzzle together. Schools need curriculums that are aligned with the state standards and reflect the state assessments. However, to be most successful, schools need curriculums that are also meaningful and relevant to their students. I tell schools all the time, "You do not have to teach *like* the test, to teach *for* the test!"

Schools are also in the constant search for more resources for their teachers, and yet have to work with budgets that are more constrained than ever. Schools need the parents to be more involved in the instruction of their children, which means more than just coming up to the school for parent-teacher conferences. The parents and the business community become much more invested in the schools when they are more actively engaged with the instructional program. School success requires that every person in the community becomes a true stakeholder in education and feels vested and responsible for the school's success. COMPASS can be the program that pulls all of these divergent pieces together.

All business-teacher learning connections are based on the teacher's curriculums. Therefore, COMPASS will help teachers get the right resources at the right time. The COWs provide a way for the community to see what the teachers are doing, and open a door for the community to participate in the instruction of their youth. Today's communications systems allow people to be in constant contact with each other. COMPASS is the communication tool that keeps the business community and the school in contact when there is valuable information to share.

TAG . . . You're It!

Head 'em Up and Move 'em Out!
Let's Get the Herd Moving in the Same Direction!

Exercise One:

For your administrative team to get started, I am going to assume that your school has COWs in place and in use. As I mentioned earlier, the staff must be comfortable with using the COWs before trying to develop learning connections with a business. If not, your first exercise as an administrative team would be to work with your staff to build your COWs and develop a few learning connections.

I mentioned several ways to generate a list of the potential businesses to participate in COMPASS on page nine. The first exercise is to have a meeting with the staff or the leadership team to discuss if your school is ready for COMPASS and, if so, to generate a list of potential business partners.

Remember to discuss and plan how the contact with particular businesses will be made, and assign personal responsibilities for those contacts. Personal responsibility should be assigned for who will make the initial contacts and who will conduct the initial presentations. The staff members involved should prepare together and conduct practice presentations to some or all of the staff.

Exercise Two:

Now it is time for the administrative team to invite a business to come in and view your COW to look for possible learning connections between the business and your curriculums. If the businesses cannot come to the school, the presentations will have to be on site at the businesses. Have the business select a color and indicate whether they want to use that color for dots, stars, or tabs to indicate potential learning connections. After the business has indicated a few possible learning connections, have the teachers pick only one at a time to discuss and develop with the business. Discussing and developing one learning connection at a time with the business partners will keep the teachers and the business from ever becoming overwhelmed.

The following are some of the questions for teachers and business personnel to consider as they work together to develop the learning connection.

- What will the lesson look like?

- What will the teachers use from the business to demonstrate the concept?

- Will it be some hard-copy example or reference?

- Will someone from the business come in to present to the students?

- Will there be a visitation to the business?

- What combination of these possibilities might be used?

Administrators should remind teachers to keep the businesses up-to-date as to the various units' progress. The teachers and students should send to the business samples of the students' work as available, and include comments from the students whenever possible. Administrators and teachers should invite the business to come watch during the unit, even if they are not going to be presenting. Finally, send a thank-you note and portfolio of sample work from the unit when it is completed.

Differentiated Staff Meetings

Staff Meetings that Rock!

As a teacher, I would dread going to staff meetings unless I knew that it was a special event—like near the holidays because I knew then there would be food at the meeting! As a coach, I would use that excuse as often as I could to get out of having to attend staff meetings, unless again, there was going to be food there. You already know two things about me, I hated staff meetings—and I love food.

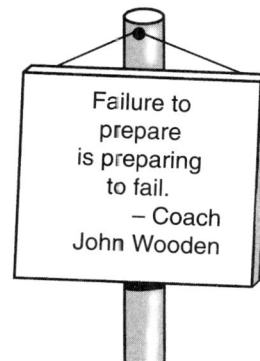

> Failure to
> prepare
> is preparing
> to fail.
> – Coach
> John Wooden

The problem with most staff meetings is that they are used for general announcements, and few of the announcements relate to all of the staff. So when the first announcement and the following discussion are about the pep rally this coming Friday, a portion of the staff tunes out because they have nothing to do with the pep rally and they know they will be in the teachers' lounge before the pep rally even starts. *(They are the teachers that always let their students go early—you know the ones.)*

Then the administrator has to try to get everyone's attention again for the next topic, and so it goes. So here are some tips for conducting a successful staff meeting.

1 **Do not bring up anything that does not engage the entire staff.** When a topic at a staff meeting does not pertain to the entire staff, not only are some staff members not involved during that topic, I have wasted their time. As a matter of fact, I have not used the administrative team's time very well either. As an administrator, I want every topic at a staff meeting to be meaningful for everyone at the meeting. If I have topics for smaller groups, then one of the administrators will meet with the small groups so that everyone at the meeting is a part of the topic at hand and actively engaged.

2 **Keep the staff actively engaged** in the topics during the staff meeting. The staff is not actively engaged when they are listening to someone talk, especially if this is all that happens during the staff meeting.

Administrators would not want any teacher to use lecture as the only instructional strategy. Why then are so many staff meetings basically a few people lecturing to the staff? Not only is using staff meetings for general announcement not very efficient, it is also a very ineffective way to communicate with the staff, or anybody for that matter. Think parent meetings.

We know that most staff meetings are mainly auditory affairs. For the staff to be actively engaged, staff meetings must also be visual and kinesthetic experiences. Administrators need to differentiate staff meetings for their staffs just as they expect teachers to differentiate classroom lessons for their students. This means that the administrative team will consider learning modalities and multiple intelligences as they plan activities for the staff to present their topics.

Administrators actually need to plan for staff meetings! This means no more picking up the topics from the secretary's desk as you leave the office and prepping for the staff meeting on the way there. I understand that planning takes time, but a well-planned staff meeting will ultimately save more time than its planning will require.

To assist administrators in planning, I have included a list of considerations and suggestions to use when preparing for differentiated staff meeting topics. Each of the considerations and suggestions is explained here. Use the abbreviated checklist on page 206. Duplicate it and encourage your administrative team to use it as they plan for staff meetings.

Considerations and Suggestions for Differentiated Staff Meeting Topics

? What presentation styles might be used to present the topic?

☐ Plan for the presentation of each topic as if you were planning to differentiate instruction in a classroom.

☐ Use auditory, kinesthetic, and visual strategies during the presentation.

☐ Use Bloom's Taxonomy and the multiple intelligences; verbal-linguistic, logical-mathematical, visual-spatial, body-kinesthetic, musical-rhythmic, interpersonal, intrapersonal, and naturalist.

? What activities *(from the word ACTIVE)* **will be used to present the topic?**

☐ Will the entire staff be doing an activity requiring a lot of movement like "forming a brain" to discuss the impact of learning styles on teaching and vice-versa? *(This activity is described in this chapter. Keep reading.)*

☐ Will the staff be in discussion groups for a jigsaw activity? How will you form the groups for the activity?

☐ Will the staff be moving between workstations? How will they get themselves into groups? How long will a group have to complete the activity at each station?

☐ How are you going to bring closure to this activity?

☐ What materials are needed to present this topic?

Using a variety of presentation styles requires a variety of materials. For example, you may need an LCD projector for PowerPoint presentations; flipcharts for brainstorming sessions; rubber balls for a group juggle; and markers, sticky notes, and file folders for a strategy-sharing activity.

☐ Are timelines going to be established as a result of this topic?

If follow-up is required, timelines should be made clear.

☐ Will assessments be required? What types of assessments?

How will you assess the success of the presentation?
Will there be other aspects of this presentation that will
require later assessments? If so, they must be established
as a part of this session.

☐ How much time is going to be required for this topic?

Allow enough time for the presentation to come to closure.
Planning differentiated presentations for staff meetings will
limit the number of topics that can be attempted at any one
staff meeting. (What you want to think here is clearly
quality over quantity.)

☐ Where will the presentation be?

Depending on the activities used in the presentations, some
venues might be more appropriate than others. So one staff
meeting might be held in the gym, while another meeting
might work better in the cafeteria.

?   ## What are the personal responsibilities?

☐ Who is going to facilitate the staff meeting?
If it is a teacher/team/department, who will make
sure they are ready to go? Will the administrative
team need to provide coverage for teachers to leave
classes to set up for their presentation?

☐ Who is going to be responsible for each of the
agenda topics?
The administrative team should invite teachers/
departments/academies/teams to present at staff
meetings on a regular basis.

☐ Who keeps the agenda/record book?

Some member of the staff or administrative team should
keep the notes from staff meetings and publish those to
the staff in a timely manner after each staff meeting. The
agenda record should be available to staff at all times in
an easily accessible place.

☐ Who will check on the meeting room?

This depends on where the staff meeting is going to take place. One administrator asked me to do an activity with his staff since I was there on a staff meeting day. I asked him if we could use the cafeteria, and he said that would be no problem. Later he announced for the staff to report to the cafeteria only to realize that several after-school tutorial programs were going on in the cafeteria.

☐ Who will set up the room (seating, projector, screen pads and pens, and so on)?

The tables and chairs do not move themselves, and it takes some time to move them. Someone needs to have the room in the required seating configuration when the staff arrives. Having staff move chairs and tables wastes valuable time.

☐ Who is going to bring any materials needed for this meeting?

Many staff meetings have been put on hold for someone to run back to the office or to a classroom to get some needed materials like: the sample test packets and/or survey forms and/or the curriculum maps and . . . you get the idea.

☐ Who will get the refreshments (very important!)?

This just might be the most critical part of all of the planning. I have found that as my reputation grew for having really good food at staff meetings, the better the attendance was. I hope it was because of all of the other planning that went into the meetings as well; but I know that food definitely helps!

☐ Who is going to be the timekeeper for the staff meeting?

Someone has to keep time for the topics and keep the staff on the timeframe for each topic.

☐ Who is going to inform the appropriate personnel staff of the staff meeting and the location?

Someone must herd the staff in the right direction for this week's staff meeting; send out emails; stop by classes; send notes around; make announcements; and put up signs in the office, in hallways, the teacher's lounge, the cafeteria, and so on.

☐ Who is going to get the give-away items for the staff meeting?

I always had items such as gift certificates from local establishments, coupons for free items at fast-food places, and other goodies like "Feel Good Days" that I will share a little later in this chapter.

Staff Meeting Planning for _____
date

Agenda Item: _____ Time Allotted: _____

Objectives: _____

_____

_____

Presentation Notes:

Planning for the Differentiated Staff Meeting Planning Topics

Note: The same planning should be used for Parent Nights.

☐ Materials needed: What materials will be required for presenting this topic? (Who will provide them? See the PRs above and below). Will the teachers need to bring anything? Who will let the teachers know and how?

☐ How much time will be needed for this topic? Limit the number of topics to allow for quality presentations.

☐ What will the presentation styles be? (Auditory/Visual/Kinesthetic and Multiple Intelligences, music/PowerPoints)

☐ Staff activity: What will the staff do? How is the staff going to be actively engaged in the explanation, application, and synthesis/closure of this topic? (For example, will the staff be engaged in: discussion groups, jig saw, goal achievement target activity, group juggle?)

☐ What will the location be for this staff meeting? Depending on the activities the staff will be participating in, different locations might be more appropriate. Changing locations also keeps the staff focused on not only when they are meeting, but also where, and what they might be doing.

☐ Assessment: How will you check for understanding? What follow-up assessment will there be regarding this topic? What are the assessment options? What feedback will be appropriate?

☐ Timeline: Will follow-up action be required? Is there a predetermined timeline for accomplishing the topic? Will a timeline need to be established as a part of the discussion/action on the topic?

**Prior to the staff meeting, roles and personal responsibilities
for the meeting should be considered and listed.
That list would include, but certainly not be limited to, the following:**

☐ Who is going to facilitate the staff meeting?

☐ Who is going to be responsible for each of the agenda topics? If it is a teacher/team/department, who will make sure they are ready to go?

☐ Who keeps the agenda /record book?

☐ Who will check on the meeting room?

☐ Who will set up the room (seating, projector, screen pads and pens, and so on)?

☐ Who is going to bring any materials needed for this meeting (test packets, survey forms, curriculum maps)?

☐ Who will get the refreshments? (Very important!)

☐ Who is going to take notes for the meeting to be published later for the staff?
(A notebook should be kept with the agenda/records of the staff meetings.)

☐ Who is going to be the timekeeper for the staff meeting?

☐ Who is going to inform the appropriate personnel staff of the staff meeting and the location?

Drawings, Feel Good Days, and More

Staff meetings should be learning experiences for the staff, but that does not mean they can't have a lot of fun as well. I have already mentioned that there should always be good food for meetings, and that will get the staff to attend. I always liked to end staff meetings with drawings for free stuff. Administrators know how teachers are about the opportunity to win free stuff: and it really doesn't matter what the free stuff is, but you do want to make it worth the wait.

It is very easy to get coupons and certificates from local businesses, and especially food establishments. Some businesses, like office supply stores and educational supply stores, will donate things to give to teachers, especially if the items have the name of the store on them. After administrators build a relationship with some stores, the business will often build into their costs the items they are going to give to the school each year. Local theatres and museums will also often give admissions to teachers. They know the teachers might then come back sometime with students.

The ultimate item I was able to give away at staff meetings was a Feel Good Day. I first heard of Feel Good Days from a keynote speaker at a conference who spoke of wishing there were "Feel Good Days" in addition to "Sick Days." That way a teacher could call the school and say that he or she just felt way too good to come to school on that day. Of course, it was funny at the time; but it gave me an idea for the ultimate item for our staff meeting drawings. I met with my administrative team and proposed we would give these special days away.

If a teacher won a "Feel Good Day," the administrative team would cover the classes for that teacher, and the teacher would have the day off. There was no cost to the district as we would not hire substitutes. The administrative team would take turns teaching the classes for the winning teacher. The rest of the administrative team liked the idea *(and I must share that the staff also really liked the idea)*. In fact, we opened the drawing to noninstructional staff as well, which means that the administrative team had opportunities to be secretaries and custodians as well as teachers. The staff member had to be present to win, so our attendance at staff meetings was always excellent. *(An added bonus: In all my years as administrator, each of my personal experiences of giving "Feel Good Days" and covering for my staff gave me insights that I could not have received in any other way.)*

Differentiated Staff Meeting Activities and Resources

Throughout the chapter, I have mentioned several valuable references to help you differentiate staff meetings. Check out the bibliography at the end of this book for more. Be sure to look for *Because You Teach, Learning to Learn, Fire Up For Learning!, Positive Classroom Management, Success with IEPS* and the companion fold-out *How to Write a Successful IEP.*

I have found some of my best activities for staff meetings in the business section of various bookstores. The business community is in a constant state of training. You will find many business books with training activities to build communication skills, conflict resolution skills, positive problem-solving skills, and customer service skills. Here are a few examples of such books from which I have pulled activities for staff meetings.

Basic Training for Trainers, Second edition,
    a handbook for new trainers
Gary Kroehnert
McGraw-Hill Book Company
ISBN 0-07-470193-2

The Big Book of Business Games; Icebreakers,
    Creativity Exercises, and Meeting Energizers
John Newstrom and Edward Scannell
McGraw-Hill
ISBN 0-07-046476-6

Imaginative Events for Training; A Trainer's Sourcebook
    of Games, Simulations, and Role-Play Exercises
Ken Jones
McGraw-Hill, Inc.
ISBN 0-07-033019-0

Team Games for Trainers
    Carolyn Nilson
    McGraw-Hill, Inc.
    ISBN 0-07-046588-6

You get the idea; every time I go into a bookstore I find new books like the ones listed above. I often have administrators tell me that they are not creative enough to come up with meaningful and motivating activities. I am letting you in on the secret that there are literally endless resources available to assist you in getting creative with staff meetings. These materials will dramatically reduce preparation time and the need for individual creativity.

Here are a couple of my favorite staff meeting activities:

★ Puzzles

In the book *Fire Up For Learning!* there is an activity called Team Puzzles. Staff Puzzle is an adaptation of Team Puzzles. So I will briefly describe the team puzzles, and explain how to make the activity a staff puzzle.

Team Puzzle

Teachers create a large "puzzle" by writing the team name on an extended piece of art paper or butcher paper. Then each student on the team decorates a piece of the puzzle. Students decorate their pieces to share information about themselves. So students write and draw things, add photographs of their families, favorite singers, friends, and pets. The team puzzle is put on display above the lockers to designate the team area, and represents the students on the team. Despite the students' various shapes, sizes, and interests, they fit together as a team.

Staff Puzzle

Each staff member in the school gets a piece of the puzzle to decorate. The teachers might put things about the subject they teach, their personal interests, their colleges, and their families. The additions to the puzzle pieces can be cumulative. Over the years, I have seen teachers add pictures of children, and then later weddings and grandchildren. When staff members retire or move, they are given their pieces of the puzzle to take with them. Imagine the impact when the administrative team places the retiring staff member's puzzle piece in a large frame surrounded by the signatures of the rest of the staff and presents it the retiree.

★ Be a Brain

As a Student Activity

Students answer questions about brain preferences by moving left or right depending on their answers. Basically the students end up sorting themselves according to brain preferences. Students who are more left-brain dominant will be standing to the left of the teacher. Students who are more right-brain dominant will be standing to the right of the teacher. Then the teacher has the students move forward to form a semi-circle which represents the human brain. The teacher then walks into the student-formed hemispheres of the brain and leads discussions about brain preferences. *(For a detailed step-by-step description, see* Fire Up for Learning!*)*

As a Staff Meeting Activity

You may want to have staff members form a single line and move right or left in response to examples of activities that might indicate brain dominance.

Once the teachers have organized themselves into groups, ask them to cross their arms. Then, have the teachers cross their arms the wrong way. *(This is very uncomfortable for everyone, and actually quite difficult for some.)*

The teachers hold their arms crossed the wrong way for this discussion. The leader will ask the teachers if they think that the way a person crosses their arms is an indication of intelligence. "If a person crosses their arms differently from you, does that mean that person is more or less likely to be a better writer, or mathematician, or artist?"

Have the teachers shake out their arms and relax them very briefly, and then cross their arms again the wrong way. While the task will still be uncomfortable, most teachers will be doing it a little more easily than in their first attempt. The idea here is that, with practice, they could all become very comfortable with crossing their arms either way. They would always naturally cross them one way, but they could switch and function very well the other way if needed.

The point you should make is that this is what we want teachers to do in their classrooms. Students come into their classes with different comfort levels with a subject and the teacher's style. Metaphorically speaking, the way some students cross their arms will fit the class naturally, and for some not so much. If the teacher can identify the learning preferences of the students, he or she can help the students learn to be more comfortable in his or her classroom. Pretty soon it will not matter which way the students cross their arms, so to speak, the teachers work with them to make them successful in any classroom setting.

TAG . . . You're It!

Planning Staff Meetings

Exercise One

The administrative team should use the planning form on page nine and plan activities for the next staff meeting. Consider the possible topics for the next staff meeting, and determine if any of them could be presented in one of the ways demonstrated in this chapter.

Exercise Two

The administrative team should brainstorm other ways to get information out so that staff meetings might be used for real presentations. Administrators know the frustrations that result when some of the staff "doesn't get the message." Administrators are often saying things to teachers and students like, "It was in the announcements. Didn't you listen to the announcements?" Remember to consider auditory, visual, and kinesthetic options, as well as the multiple intelligences. Give teachers a chance to receive and "experience" the general announcements differently.

Exercise Three

Using the experience of exercise two, involve interested staff members and consider what options might be available for delivering announcements to the students.

Chapter 10

Differentiated Leadership for the Whole School

The Cognaffective School

Do not run to your Webster's Dictionary! This is an example of a word I made up, but I have given a great deal of thought to this word. *Cognaffective* is my combination of the words *cognitive* and *affective*, and is meant to demonstrate the interaction between the development of cognitive skills in conjunction with affective skills. All of the strategies presented in this book so far have concentrated on balancing the cognitive and affective domains. This chapter brings that balance into focus.

> Effective leaders must recognize the interaction between the development of cognitive skills and affective skills.

Did you notice that the cognitive skills and the affective skills were always dependent on each other? For example, in the curriculum mapping chapter, teachers completed tasks to:

- build the curriculum maps using curriculum guides,

- color-code the curriculum maps,

- ensure curriculum alignment with state standards within each content area,

- correlate the state assessment items with specific units,

- correlate the district pacing guide with the curriculum maps,

- correlate unit assessments with state assessment items, and

- identify skill sets from their content area for use in other content areas.

These jobs reflect the **cognitive** tasks of the curriculum mapping process, and these tasks, of course, require corresponding cognitive skills. Most teachers are highly trained, very competent, and comfortable with these tasks.

However, for the curriculum mapping to have real impact on instruction and student performance, teachers had to complete several additional tasks. One important task was finding and developing interdisciplinary learning connections. To do this teachers had to

- write notes to other teachers indicating possible learning connections,

- discuss skills from their area with a teacher from another content area,

- share activities from their class with teachers of other subjects,

- give students extra credit for work done in other classes,

- coordinate homework with the other teacher,

- share worksheets and assessments they have developed with teachers from other disciplines,

- look for multiple learning connections, and

- coordinate ongoing interdisciplinary student projects with multiple teachers from multiple disciplines.

(As you know from the curriculum development chapter, this is just the tip of the proverbial iceberg!)

All of the tasks in the second list require **affective** skills. Teachers had to collaborate, share ideas, share activities, discuss skills from other areas as well as their own with teachers, give to others, work well with teachers from other content areas, be organized, be good listeners, be good questioners, be good communicators, be motivators, and so much more! While teachers are very good at the cognitive skills, the same is not always true of the affective skills. In fact, some teachers will tell administrators pretty quickly that they cannot work with _____.
(Fill in the blank with a teacher's name in the building.)

(This is what I believe.) A focus on the cognitive skills alone often results in "drill and kill" types of direct instruction with too many worksheets and lectures. There are practice tests for the practice tests for the real tests. When affective skills are brought into the teaching equation, teachers take into consideration students' learning styles and will work to differentiate instruction and

assessment. In a strictly cognitive situation, the teacher is the expert presenter of the knowledge, and the student is mostly responsible for getting that knowledge regardless of how it is presented. Think of college and graduate school as having a mostly cognitive orientation. On the opposite side, in a strictly affective setting, the only concern would be students' well-being and self-esteem, with little concern given to how much cognitive development there is, as long as students "feel good" about themselves.

Affective skills, such as being able to focus and listen, are important for developing the skills of learning the branches of government and their functions. Understanding roles and responsibilities and how to work well in groups is critical to being successful in lab settings or group projects. Arriving on time and prepared for class is a basic prerequisite to being successful in any class. This list could go on, and in fact, it is the generation of this list that I use to define the affective skills that should be the foundation of any advisory program.

In the *cognaffective school*, the administrative team puts equal emphasis on the development of the cognitive skills and the affective skills of the staff and the students. True differentiated leadership means the leaders run a cognaffective school. I do not know many educators that would argue against the need for affective skills for students. What I am saying here, is that it is important for administrators to work to develop their teachers' affective skills if they want the most productive school possible.

Consider the graph on page 216 with affective skill development being represented on the horizontal axis and cognitive skill development being represented on the vertical axis. In quadrant I, you see the cognaffective schools where an equal emphasis is placed on both cognitive skill development and affective skill development. These are schools where it truly is fun to learn, and the teachers and students share the responsibility for learning. In quadrants II, III, and IV you see the results of placing increased or decreased emphasis on development of both cognitive and affective skills.

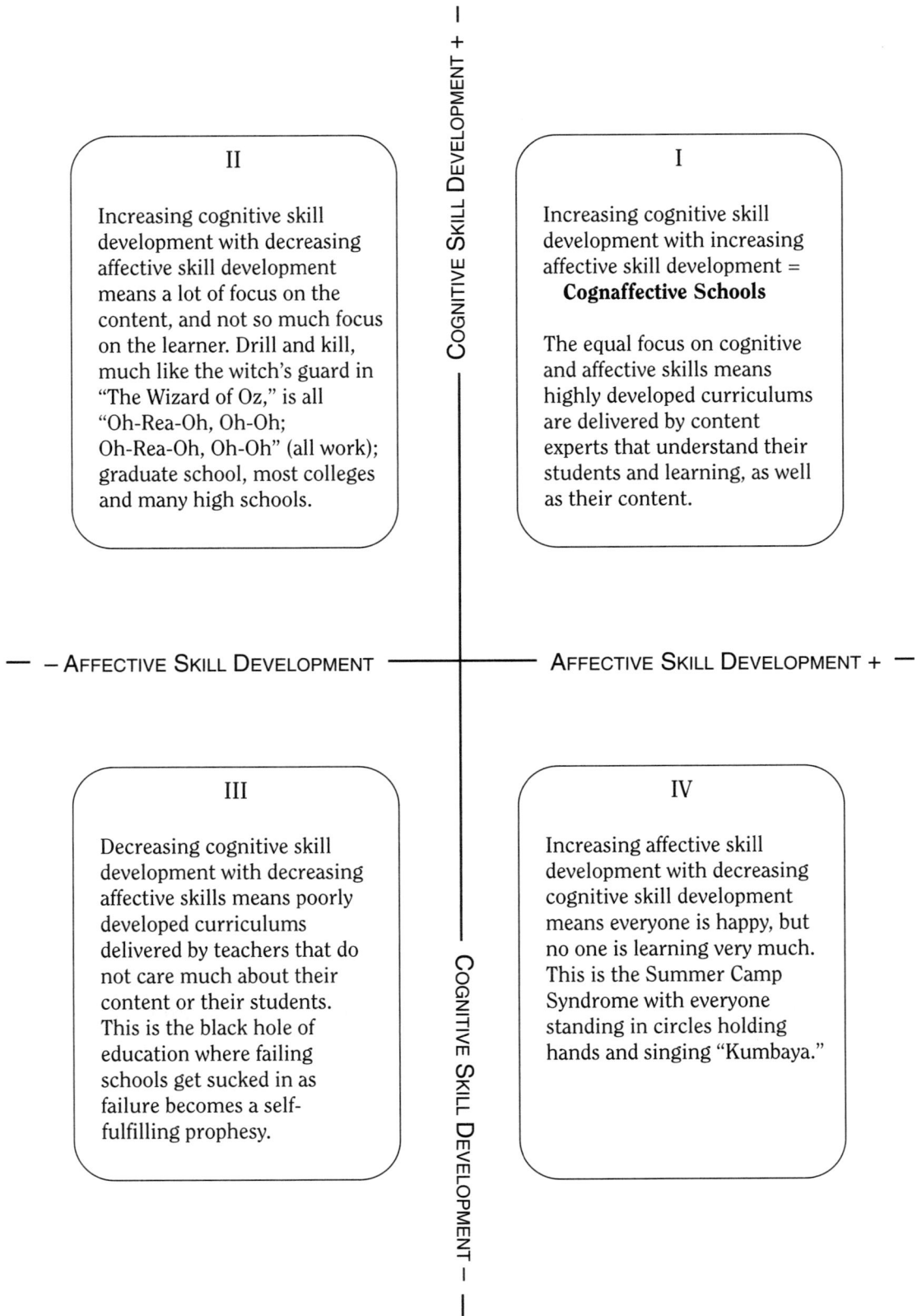

COGNITIVE SKILL DEVELOPMENT +

II

Increasing cognitive skill development with decreasing affective skill development means a lot of focus on the content, and not so much focus on the learner. Drill and kill, much like the witch's guard in "The Wizard of Oz," is all "Oh-Rea-Oh, Oh-Oh; Oh-Rea-Oh, Oh-Oh" (all work); graduate school, most colleges and many high schools.

I

Increasing cognitive skill development with increasing affective skill development = **Cognaffective Schools**

The equal focus on cognitive and affective skills means highly developed curriculums are delivered by content experts that understand their students and learning, as well as their content.

— − AFFECTIVE SKILL DEVELOPMENT ——————— AFFECTIVE SKILL DEVELOPMENT + —

III

Decreasing cognitive skill development with decreasing affective skills means poorly developed curriculums delivered by teachers that do not care much about their content or their students. This is the black hole of education where failing schools get sucked in as failure becomes a self-fulfilling prophesy.

IV

Increasing affective skill development with decreasing cognitive skill development means everyone is happy, but no one is learning very much. This is the Summer Camp Syndrome with everyone standing in circles holding hands and singing "Kumbaya."

COGNITIVE SKILL DEVELOPMENT − −

In the book *Ten Steps to a Learning Organization*, the goal of creating a learning organization is accomplished as much with affective skills as it is with cognitive skills. The book is about developing a cognaffective learning organization.

I want all administrators to remember that developing cognitive skills and developing affective skills it is not an either/or choice. Some students learn *because of* what teachers do in the classroom, and some students learn *in spite of* what teachers do in the classroom. Providing differentiated learning ensures that learning almost always occurs because of what teachers do, and, very rarely, in spite of what they do in the classroom. For differentiated learning to happen, teachers must bring at least as much, if not even more, of their affective skillset to the classroom as they do their content knowledge.

Some teachers in schools are able to be great teachers because of what the administrative team does, and some are able to be great teachers in spite of what the administrative team does. The purpose of this book is to help administrative teams ensure that successful teaching in their buildings is almost always because of what they do, and not in spite of what they do. Just as in the classroom for the teachers, it will be the affective skills that administrators must bring to schools, and which they must help teachers develop; that will be key to their teachers' success, just as much, if not even more than their knowledge of state assessment standards or scheduling techniques.

It is the constant attention to both the cognitive side and the affective side of each concept, idea, and program that will maximize the opportunities available. The programs and strategies that have been shared in this book are all designed to help teachers build and use both cognitive and affective skills. A process like the curriculum mapping one starts with very cognitive tasks, and then, as teachers begin collaborating in small steps, builds affective skills. The result is an interdisciplinary curriculum that is incredibly rigorous with state standards cross-referenced in all content areas.

Parent/teacher conferences are another great example of needing a blend of cognitive skills and affective skills. For example, one teacher feels she is ready for her meeting with a parent. She has every action and reaction of the student documented (almost verbatim), every grade for every assignment in her grade book, every absence and every tardy accounted for, and of course, she has her copies of the referrals she has written for the student. This teacher put effort into being as cognitively prepared for this meeting as is possible. However, *(and administrators know where I am going here)* if she does not bring the necessary affective skills, it really does not matter how much information she brings to the meeting.

The teacher has to have good communication skills, part of which means being a very good listener; being able to put the parent at ease and avoid getting the parent on the defensive; demonstrating empathy for the parent; being able to paraphrase for understanding; and demonstrating positive body language. Parent meetings are successful only if teachers are prepared with the appropriate information, **and** if they know how to conduct a good meeting. Administrators have to help teachers understand that being prepared for a parent meeting means preparing cognitively and affectively.

The diagram on page 219 shows that cognaffective schools are those that pay close attention to developing the cognitive and affective skills of the teachers. Differentiated leadership means that leaders provide strategies, systems, and every opportunity to bring the cognitive and the affective together in the school. Use the practical, easy-to-implement strategies and systems in this book to actively engage your staff in developing and using both their cognitive and affective skills.

Cognitive Focus

- Teachers know their subjects and are content experts
- Teachers know the state standards
- Teachers know the Student Manual/Code of Conduct
- Discipline is mostly consequence based
- Departmental curriculum development
- Curriculum alignment with state standards
- Instruction is driven by curriculum pacing guide
- Assessment by standardized assessments
- Individual lesson planning
- Teacher is presenter of knowledge and not necessarily a motivator
- Grade is seen as motivation
- Rigorous
- Standard master schedule
- Standard use of referrals
- Mostly individual lesson planning
- Grades are the primary reward system (honor roll, principal's list, and so on.)

Cognaffective Schools

- Teachers know their students as well as their subjects.
- Discipline is handled with proactive strategies as well as with consequences.
- As much focus on positive reinforcements as consequences
- Teachers collaborate across content areas to develop instruction and assessment options.
- Teachers understand learning, use many motivators, and differentiate instruction and assessment.
- Advisory Program teaches students affective student skills.
- There are as many positive parent contacts as negative parent contacts.
- Teachers use flexible instructional time to modify for common or authentic assessments.
- Attention is paid to school climate and school pride.
- Rigorous program delivered by caring teachers and administrators.
- And so on—always balancing the cognitive with the affective!

Affective Focus

- Teachers know their students
- Discipline is more positive reinforcement-based
- Interdisciplinary curriculum development
- Instruction is based on student understanding
- Teachers understand learning and regularly modify instructional strategies (learning modalities, Multiple Intelligences, and so on.)
- Teachers have people skills
- Teachers use assessment options
- Teachers make a lot of parent contacts
- Much teacher collaboration
- Collaborative lesson planning
- Teacher is motivator
- Metacognition is taught
- Referral reviews
- Thumbs Meetings
- Reward/positive reinforcement systems
- COWs for interdisciplinary curriculum development
- Advisory programs
- Flexible schedule
- Assessment options

TAG . . . You're It!

Final Exercise

The administrative team should brainstorm what descriptors would complete this thought: as a leader, I could work with any teacher if the teacher could and/or would do _____, _____, _____, and . . . . The idea is to fill in the blanks with as many descriptors of what you need a teacher to do as possible. Try to imagine all of the various scenarios in which an administrator might work with or help a teacher, including, but certainly not limited to, classroom instruction, discipline, committee work, parent meetings and involvement, hallway, and other area supervisions.

Now consider the same thought, substituting the word "leader" with "colleague," and filling in the blanks as if you were a colleague of a teacher; add those descriptors to your list. Now consider the same thought as above, substituting the word "leader" with "parent," and filling in the blanks as if you were the parent of a student in a teacher's class.

Finally *(I'm sure you know what is coming next)*, consider the same thought as above, substituting the word "student" for "leader." Fill in the blanks as if you were a student of a teacher, and add those descriptors to your list.

You and your administrative team have just completed a list of the descriptors of the skills of your "dream" teacher. Now divide the list into *Cognitive Skills* and *Affective Skills*. Which list is longer? What can the administrative team do to help teachers continue to develop all of the skills on the lists? The idea is to consider this list when designing in-services and professional development.

Developing an environment where all of the skills of the combined lists are valued and improved upon continually and equilaterally defines **differentiated leadership**!

References

George, Dr. Paul. *The Exemplary High School.*

Goleman, Daniel. *Emotional Intelligence* (1995) A Bantam Book.

Jacobe, H. H. *Mapping the Big Picture: Integrating Curriculum and Assessment K-12* (1997) Alexandria, VA. Association for Supervision and Curriculum Development.

Kline, Peter and Bernard Saunders. *Ten Steps to a Learning Organization* (1993) Great Ocean Publishers, Inc.

Kriegel, Robert J. *If it Ain't Broke . . . Break It!—and Other Unconventional Wisdom for a Changing Business World* (1991) Warner Books, Inc.

Kriegel, Robert J. *Sacred Cows Make The Best Burgers—Developing Change-Ready People and Organizations* (1996) Warner Books Inc.

McNally, David. *Even Eagles Need A Push—Learning to Soar in a Changing World* Dell Publishing.

Pink, Daniel H. *A Whole New Mind* (2006) The Berkley Publishing Group.

Senge, Peter M. *The Fifth Discipline—The Art & Science of The Learning Organization* (1994) Currency Doubleday.

Udelofen, S. *Keys To Curriculum Mapping: Strategies And Tools To Make It Work.* Thousand Oaks, CA: Corwin Press.

From Incentive Publications

Advisory Plus

Because You Teach

Curriculum and Project Planner

Fire Up For Learning!

Get Fit!

If You Don't Feed The Teachers They Eat the Kids

Learning to Learn

WOW, What A Team!

From the NMSA

Anfara, Vincent and Sandra Stacki. *Middle School Curriculum, Instruction, and Assessment* (2002).

Caskey, Miki. *Making a Difference: Action Research in Middle Level Education* (2005).

Research and Resource in Support of This We Believe (2003).

Turning Points 2000: Education Adolescents in the 21st Century.